THE FIRST CIVILIZATIONS

Giovanni Caselli

PETER BEDRICK BOOKS

NEW YORK

HISTORY OF EVERYDAY THINGS

The First Civilizations
Giovanni Caselli
ISBN 0-911745-59-9 hc LE

"The book(s) on the short list of recommended
readings were carefully chosen for their
accuracy and the educational level addressed."
—*Science Books & Films*

The Roman Empire
Giovanni Caselli
ISBN 0-911745-58-0 hc LE

"Tremendously useful at the elementary
through college levels ..."
—*New England Classical Newsletter*

The Middle Ages
Giovanni Caselli
ISBN 0-87226-263-4 pb
ISBN 0-87226-176-X hc LE

"Excellent"—*School Library Journal*

The Renaissance
Giovanni Caselli
ISBN 0-87226-050-X hc LE

"It is an excellent reference and worthy
investment by secondary school and college
libraries ... gloriously and meticulously illustrated ..."
—*Science Books & Films*

Published by
Peter Bedrick Books
2112 Broadway
New York, NY 10023

Published by agreement with Simon & Schuster Young Books,
Simon & Schuster Ltd, Hemel Hempstead, England

Library of Congress Cataloging-in-Publication Data
Caselli, Giovanni, fl. 1976.
    The first civilizations.
    Bibliography: p.
    Summary: Traces the early history of civilization from the first
toolmakers of four million years ago through the Greeks of the fifth
century B.C.
    1. Civilization, Ancient—Juvenile literature. 2. Man,
Prehistoric—Juvenile literature. [1. Civilization, Ancient. 2. Man,
Prehistoric] I. Title.
CB311.C346   1985   930   84-6179

ISBN 0-911745-59-9

Printed in Hong Kong by Wing King Tong Ltd.

Sixth printing 1995

Introduction

Civilization is a difficult word to define. Man's domestication of plants and animals was an enormous step forward in the evolution of human culture, for example, but agriculture alone cannot, by itself, account for the rise of civilization. Civilization means much more than growing crops and raising animals; it means more than the invention of writing or the wheel. The early civilizations of the Middle East tended to have extensive irrigation which provided their societies not only with the certainty of feeding themselves, but also allowed them to produce large surpluses of food. This freed men to work as craftsmen, rather than having to work on the land all the time to produce enough food.

Surplus crops and the goods produced by the craftsmen could be traded; this required book-keeping which, together with taxation and the need to keep records, led to the development of writing. Trade grew increasingly more important and sea and land transport developed, allowing contacts between different cultures. Ancient Egypt developed a sophisticated calendar in order to organize its agriculture to tie in with the regular floods of the Nile. All these are aspects of civilization

No one factor, however, can account for the rise of what we call civilized society. Each civilization represents an adaptation to a unique set of circumstances. But there is one thing that all civilizations would seem to have in common and that is a stratified society, a degree of specialization: rulers, administrators, soldiers, priests, traders, artisans and peasants. There is no civilization without at least two classes of people: the rich and the poor. This, it seems, is the price mankind has to pay for being civilized.

Contents

The Earliest Toolmakers
4,000,000 – 35,000 years ago   4

The Ice Age Hunters
35,000 – 10,000 years ago   8

The Fisher-Hunters
12,000 – 7,000 years ago   12

Çatal Hüyük: The First City
9,000 years ago   16

The First Food Producers
7,000 – 3,000 years ago   20

The Craftsmen of Egypt
4,500 years ago   24

Minoan Crete
3,500 years ago   28

People of the North
3,200 years ago   32

A Chinese Pavilion
3,000 years ago   36

The Etruscans
2,600 years ago   40

The Greeks at Home
2,400 years ago   44

A brief chronology   48
Booklist   48

The earliest toolmakers

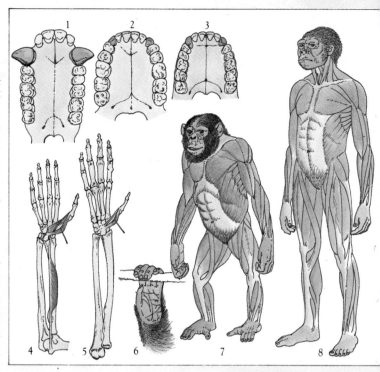

Scientific research has shown that the modern human being *(Homo sapiens)* is closely related to the great apes – gorillas, chimpanzees, orang-utans and gibbons. Scientists describe man and these apes as primates. The basic differences between man and the other primates are both behaviourial and anatomical. They include: the ability to walk upright all the time, tool-making, language, culture and a sense of family kinship within a more complex social organisation.

The need for tools

There are many theories about the first tools and why they were made. The earliest were probably just sticks which our ancestors used to reach things that were otherwise out of reach. But stone tools may first have been used to help older members of a group. If teeth had been lost or worn down so much that chewing tough food was difficult, stone tools to cut up or crush the food would make eating much easier. Their use as substitute teeth, originally restricted to the old, would then have spread throughout the group.

Who made the first tools?

Making simple stone tools does not require much intelligence. Modern apes, particularly chimpanzees, often make and use simple tools. However, using the yardstick that a large brain in relation to the size of the body is a sign of intelligence, the first tool-makers were probably primates who lived in Africa sometime between five and one million years ago. Scientists call them *Australopithecus*.

Between three and one million years ago different types of *Australopithecus* developed in different parts of Africa. But another primate, which scientists call *Homo habilis*, also appeared. *Homo habilis*, which is Latin for 'handyman', certainly made tools. He was also much more closely related to modern man than *Australopithecus*.

Homo erectus first appeared about one and a half million years ago. He made efficient tools and built shelters and probably used fire.

The Stone Age

The period scientists call the Stone Age gets its name from the fact that most tools were made of stone. The earliest Stone Age tools were made by *Homo erectus*. They were just stones with a few flakes knocked off to make a rough cutting edge.

Slowly these tools improved and thousands of years later the hand axe appeared. This efficient tool was used for everything – from skinning dead animals to digging holes. Archaeologists believe that this development of toolmaking ability closely parallels the physical evolution of man.

A common ancestor
Similarities between the anatomy of man and the apes show that the two species had a common ancestor.
1 The upper jaw of a gorilla.
2 The top jaw of *Ramapithecus*, who may have been an ancestor of both man and apes.
3 The upper jaw of a modern human. The incisor teeth are in blue, canines in red and molars in green.
4 A human forearm.
5 Forearm of a chimpanzee. Although superficially alike, the human thumb can be moved independently of the other fingers and has an extra muscle, making it stronger.
6 The hand of a chimp is good for swinging through trees, but not for handling objects with precision.
7 The muscular structure of a chimp.
8 The muscular structure of *Homo habilis*, the earliest known hominid.
9 The teeth and jaws of a baboon.
10 The teeth of a chimp. Both these animals use their teeth as tools and weapons.
11 Early humans did not have the same powerful jaws as other apes. As their teeth became worn down, they may have used stone tools to cut up their food.
12 Man uses tools more than any other living creature, but he is not the only one to do so. Chimpanzees often use a stick to dig termites out of their mounds.
13 The digging stick, for digging up edible roots, may have been man's first tool. Did he copy the chimps?

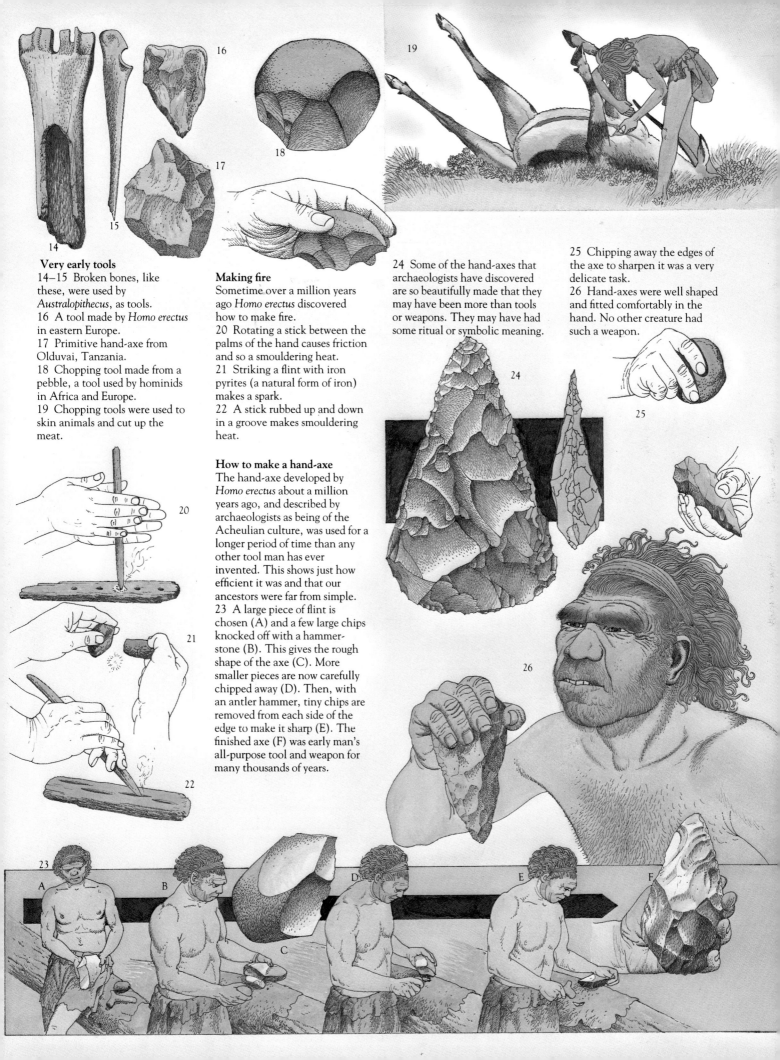

Very early tools

14–15 Broken bones, like these, were used by *Australopithecus*, as tools.

16 A tool made by *Homo erectus* in eastern Europe.

17 Primitive hand-axe from Olduvai, Tanzania.

18 Chopping tool made from a pebble, a tool used by hominids in Africa and Europe.

19 Chopping tools were used to skin animals and cut up the meat.

Making fire

Sometime over a million years ago *Homo erectus* discovered how to make fire.

20 Rotating a stick between the palms of the hand causes friction and so a smouldering heat.

21 Striking a flint with iron pyrites (a natural form of iron) makes a spark.

22 A stick rubbed up and down in a groove makes smouldering heat.

How to make a hand-axe

The hand-axe developed by *Homo erectus* about a million years ago, and described by archaeologists as being of the Acheulian culture, was used for a longer period of time than any other tool man has ever invented. This shows just how efficient it was and that our ancestors were far from simple.

23 A large piece of flint is chosen (A) and a few large chips knocked off with a hammer-stone (B). This gives the rough shape of the axe (C). More smaller pieces are now carefully chipped away (D). Then, with an antler hammer, tiny chips are removed from each side of the edge to make it sharp (E). The finished axe (F) was early man's all-purpose tool and weapon for many thousands of years.

24 Some of the hand-axes that archaeologists have discovered are so beautifully made that they may have been more than tools or weapons. They may have had some ritual or symbolic meaning.

25 Chipping away the edges of the axe to sharpen it was a very delicate task.

26 Hand-axes were well shaped and fitted comfortably in the hand. No other creature had such a weapon.

△ **Homes for early man**

1 Diagrammatic reconstruction of a hut found by archaeologists at Terra Amata, near Nice in France. The structure, over 10 metres long, was probably built by *Homo erectus*.

2 Caves made good homes for early man, as the remains of tools and animal bones found in them show. From the evidence found in the cave of La Grotte du Lazaret, France, it would seem skin tents were sometimes used inside the cave.

Tools and weapons

3 Wooden spears were important hunting weapons for *Homo erectus*. They were often made from the very hard yew wood and their sharpened tips were held in fire to harden them even more. Spears like this have been found in England and Germany.

4 Elephants were one of the large game animals which were common in Europe a few million years ago. This scene is a reconstruction of evidence found by archaeologists in Italy dating to about 70,000 years ago. A group of Neanderthal men had prepared a trap for an elephant which they managed to separate from the main herd. Once in the pit, the elephant was quite easy to kill with stone-tipped or fire-hardened spears.

◁ Although many of the tools made by early man have survived, we cannot always be sure how they were used. These are tools made by *Homo erectus*: A core from which small pieces of flint have been chipped; B side scraper; C blade tool; D long sharp shaped blade; E end scraper (the scraping edge was at the end of the tool, not at the side as in B); F-G small sharp point tools.

▷ Three different types of stone spear points made and used by Neanderthal man. Like the tools shown on the left, these were found in France.

Early hunters in Europe

Homo sapiens, which is the scientific name for modern man, probably first lived in Europe about 300,000 years ago. Hunting was their way of life, and groups made up of several families followed the great herds of wild animals which roamed across Europe. Archaeological evidence shows that these early ancestors of ours were skilful hunters. In Spain, at Toralba and Ambrona, bones found in the remains of prehistoric bogs show that scores of elephants and rhinos were driven into the bogs to be killed.

At Terra Amata, near Nice in France, the remains of an oval hut have been discovered. It may be the first building made by man in Europe. The hut was used for a few days each year by hunters.

New types of tool

Throughout this time the hand-axe became ever more refined and efficient. Even the small flakes which were struck off the main flint from which the axe was being made were turned into tools. Scientists call these small tools 'flake tools'.

The reason that archaeologists know quite a lot about tools of this period is that so many have survived. This is partly because our ancestors had begun to bury their dead, and with the body were often buried the possessions used in life.

Neanderthal Man

Neanderthal Man is a variety of *Homo sapiens* that dominated Europe, North Africa and western Asia from around 150,000 to 31,000 years ago. The name comes from the valley of the river Neander, in Germany, where the first fossil remains of this type of early man were discovered in 1856.

The climate of Europe at this time was much colder than it is now. To cope with these conditions, Neanderthal people were short and stocky – rather like the Lapps today.

Like his immediate ancestors, Neanderthal Man was a big game hunter, but the variety and quality of his tools suggest that he had a much more complex culture.

Then, around 31,000 years ago, Neanderthal Man was quite rapidly replaced by really modern men, although there is no evidence to show why this happened.

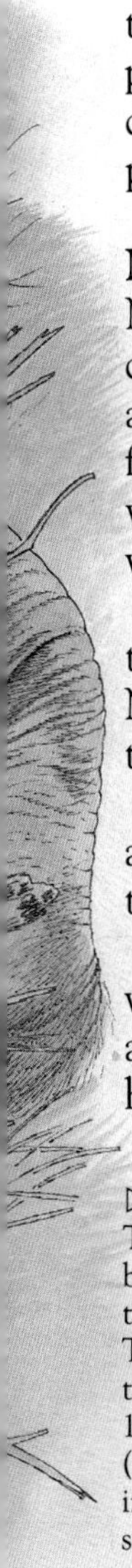

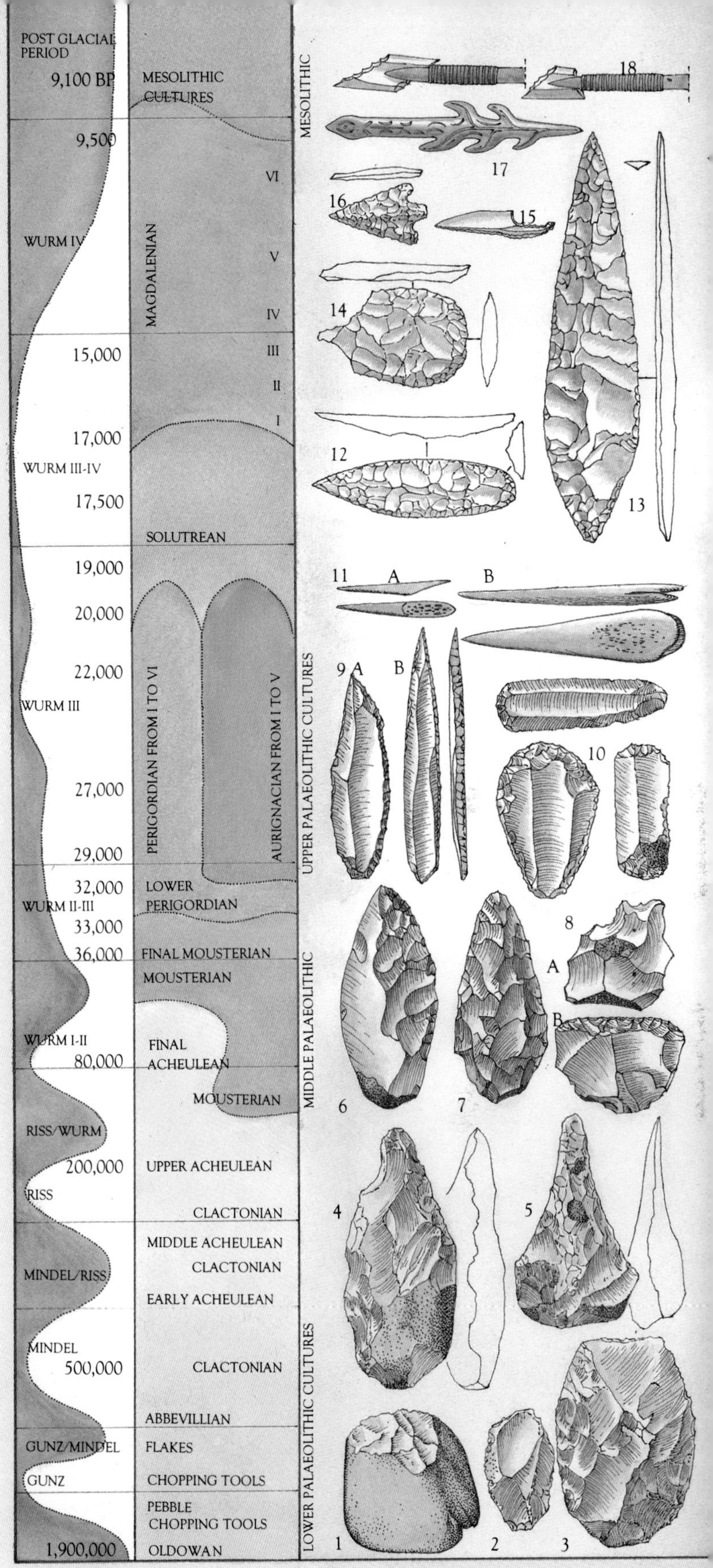

POST GLACIAL PERIOD	MESOLITHIC CULTURES	MESOLITHIC	
9,100 BP			
9,500	VI		
WURM IV	MAGDALENIAN V		
	IV		
15,000	III		
	II		
17,000	I		
WURM III-IV			
17,500	SOLUTREAN		
19,000			
20,000			
22,000	PERIGORDIAN FROM I TO VI / AURIGNACIAN FROM I TO V	UPPER PALAEOLITHIC CULTURES	
WURM III			
27,000			
29,000			
32,000	LOWER PERIGORDIAN		
WURM II-III 33,000			
36,000	FINAL MOUSTERIAN		
	MOUSTERIAN	MIDDLE PALAEOLITHIC	
WURM I-II 80,000	FINAL ACHEULEAN		
	MOUSTERIAN		
RISS/WURM 200,000	UPPER ACHEULEAN		
RISS	CLACTONIAN		
	MIDDLE ACHEULEAN CLACTONIAN		
MINDEL/RISS	EARLY ACHEULEAN		
MINDEL 500,000	CLACTONIAN	LOWER PALAEOLITHIC CULTURES	
	ABBEVILLIAN		
GUNZ/MINDEL	FLAKES		
GUNZ	CHOPPING TOOLS		
	PEBBLE CHOPPING TOOLS		
1,900,000	OLDOWAN		

▷ **How tools developed**
This chart shows how stone and bone artefacts developed throughout the Old Stone Age. The left-hand column shows the times of the glacial periods from 1,900,000 (*bottom*) to 9,100 (*top*) years ago. The white areas indicate times of cold. The second column shows the sequence of the principal European cultures.

The third column shows how stone tools developed, from crude stones made nearly 2 million years ago to beautifully sculpted, highly efficient tools of about 9,000 years ago.

1 Basalt pebble tool, Olduvai Gorge, Tanzania.
2 Clactonian flake, England.
3 Multi-purpose cleaver.
4 Primitive hand-axe, England.
5 Acheulian hand-axe.
6-7 Leaf points, Mousterian period, France.
8 A denticulated tool, B transverse scraper.
9 A Chatelperonnian knife, B Gravettian point, both French.
10 Three end scrapers.
11 A-B Aurignacian bone points.
12 Lower Solutrean leaf point.
13-14 Upper Solutrean end-scraper.
15-16 Solutrean points, Spain.
17 Magdalenian bone harpoon.
18 Mesolithic arrows.

The Ice Age hunters

The Old Stone Age is divided into three main periods – Lower, Middle and Upper Palaeolithic. (Palaeolithic comes from the Greek words for 'ancient' and 'stone'.)

The Upper Palaeolithic, the final period, lasted from about 37,000 to about 10,000 years ago. During this time the first completely modern type of *Homo sapiens* appeared in Europe. Archaeologists call these people Cro-Magnon, after the site in France where they were first studied.

Cro-Magnon Man and his tools

Cro-Magnon people were very skilful craftsmen. The tools they made were better and more efficient than any made by earlier men. Blade tools replaced the old flaked stone tools, and tools made of bone became increasingly common.

Because of variations in the tools made by Cro-Magnon people, archaeologists divide the Upper Palaeolithic into different phases. The most important of these phases are the Aurignacian, Gravettian, Solutrean and Magdalenian.

It is difficult to say exactly when each period began or ended because the rate of change varied from one part of Europe to another, so they often overlapped. But the *Aurignacian* lasted roughly from 37,000 to 30,000 years ago in western Europe and until 10,000 years ago in eastern Europe.

The *Gravettian* began around 29,000 years ago in western Europe and ended there about 20,000 years ago, although it, too, lasted until about 10,000 years ago in eastern Europe.

The *Solutrean*, which developed in central France, spread from there throughout southwestern France to Spain, lasting from around 21,000 to 16,000 years ago.

The *Magdalenian*, which started in France around 16,000 years ago spread throughout central Europe until it was replaced by the Mesolithic, or Middle Stone Age, about 8,000 years ago.

A hunter's life

The climate of Europe was colder in Palaeolithic times than it is today: this was the time of one of the great Ice Ages. But Magdalenian hunters did not have too hard a life. Great herds of reindeer, red deer and horses roamed across Europe and provided plenty of food.

The people usually lived in tents made out of the skins of the animals they had caught. Sometimes, however, they made their homes in caves. But tents were more convenient, as they could be transported easily as the hunters followed the herds of game animals.

The animal carcasses provided most necessities, and Cro-Magnon man became adept at using even animal bones to make a number of fine and useful tools.

Ice Age homes
▷ Archaeological ground plan of a tent floor found in France: A seat; B hearth; C living area; D sleeping area. The red indicates red ochre, often associated with campsites at this time.
▽ Reconstruction of how archaeologists think that an ice age hunters' camp may have looked. The skin-covered tents were built in much the same way as the North American Indians built theirs many centuries later.

An Ice Age camp

Bone needles
△ Three of the many bone needles found in Upper Palaeolithic sites. They are shown half actual size. A is a close-up of the needle's eye.
▷1 Woman sewing a wolfskin boot.
2 Making a bone needle: A the 'burins', flint tools with which the needles were made; B cutting two grooves in a reindeer bone to make a splinter; C the bone splinter; D the point of the burin is rotated to drill the eye of the needle; E smoothing the sides of the needle with a serrated flint tool; F the needle is finished by turning it in grooves made in a sandstone block.

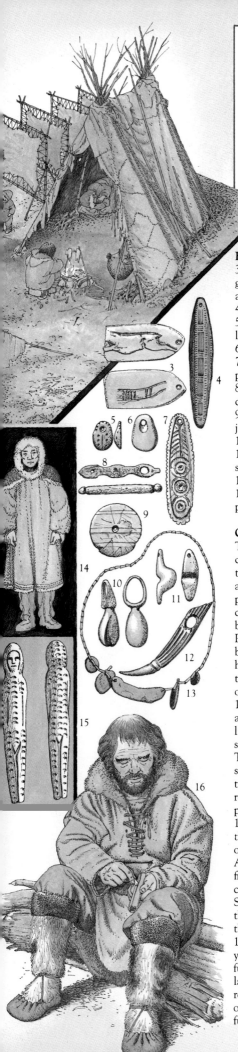

Bone ornaments
3 Engraved pendant with a galloping reindeer on one side and a sledge on the other.
4 A large engraved pendant.
5 Small pendant depicting a ladybird.
6 Small ivory pendant.
7 'Churinga' or 'bull roarer', probably used in religious rituals.
8 Bone brooches used to fasten clothes.
9 Small disc, perhaps a piece of jewellery.
10 Ring or pendant.
11 Pendant in the form of a stylized woman.
12 Decorated piece of antler.
13 Necklace of teeth and perforated pebbles.

Clothing
The soft materials from which clothing is made seldom survive to show archaeologists how our ancestors dressed. Sometimes paintings give evidence of the clothes worn at a certain period, but the only painting from Palaeolithic times is of little help because, when it does show humans, they are dressed for taking part in special rituals, not ordinary everyday activities.
14 Sometimes archaeologists are lucky enough to find people living today in conditions very similar to those of our ancestors. The Samoyeds of Soviet Siberia, shown here, live in the cold tundra area and herd and hunt reindeer, just as the Palaeolithic peoples probably did.
15 Several ivory figurines like this one have been found in sites of about 8-10,000 years ago. Although highly stylized, the figure is obviously wearing a close-fitting hood like the Samoyed's (above), so perhaps the other clothes were similar to this.
16 A man living about 10,000 years ago may have dressed in furs like this. There were still large herds of game animals roaming across Europe, so obtaining a good supply of warm furs was not difficult.

△ Different types of tent
Palaeolithic hunters were nomads so they did not need permanent homes. Tents were easy to erect and pack up.
17 Plan and reconstruction of a large tent which was really three in one, each with its own fire, living and (in red) sleeping areas.

△ Flint technology
21 Two views of a flint scraper. These tools were used mainly for getting flesh off skins.
22 Palaeolithic peoples may have fixed handles to them.
23 Reconstruction of a Magdalenian woman dressing skins with a scraper based on the Samoyed practice.
24 Flint burins (for making needles).
25 Burin hafted into a bone socket.

18 Square tent with its ground plan.
19 Double tent and its plan.
20 A large tent belonging to reindeer hunters in Germany
All these tents belonged to people of the Magdalenian culture in western Europe. The refuse they left, bones, tools etc, show us where they were.

△ The making of a flint saw tool:
A two views of the finished tool;
B a flint is held on a working platform and struck to obtain a flake; C the flake, which is already quite sharp, is held on a wooden block and its edges chipped with an antler tool to make a series of small and very sharp serrations; D once this has been done, the blade may be hafted like this; E another way of hafting a cutting blade.

A new hunting weapon

The most important tool developed during the Upper Palaeolithic period was the barbed harpoon. It was probably first made in the south of France about 16,000 years ago. It was made of bone or antler and made hunting far more efficient because the animal straining on the line attached to the harpoon's head could not get free and escape. The use of the barbed harpoon spread to Africa, Western Asia, the Far East, the Americas and Australia.

Throwing the harpoon

The spear-thrower was also invented about this time. It was used with the harpoon, as the large picture below shows, and helped the hunter to throw his harpoon even further. It was used until the invention of the bow and arrow, probably about 10,000 years ago, and greatly increased man's hunting efficiency.

The spear-thrower was also used by North American Indians until they discovered the bow and arrow. Some of the tribes of Aborigines in the remotest parts of Australia still use the spear-thrower. The bow and arrow are better weapons, however, and superseded the spear-thrower, because they enable an arrow to cover a greater distance more quickly than a spear or harpoon.

The first artists

The people of the Palaeolithic time were marvellous artists as well as good hunters. There are many caves which were painted at this time with pictures of deer, elephants and other game animals. Two of the finest are at Lascaux in southern France and Altamira in northern Spain.

The pictures found there seem to suggest that the painting was not just done for fun. Instead it may have formed part of a ritual to try and ensure good hunting, to make sure there were many herds of animals to provide food and clothing for the tribesmen. The finest paintings date to between 15,000 and 11,000 years ago. Painting them in the darkness of the caves must have required a great deal of skill.

Painting was not the only art of this time. Quite a few caves also have sculptures of animals in them. Archaeologists have also found many bones with patterns engraved on them dating from this period. No-one knows what these were for. They may possibly have been ornaments, but they were more likely a type of calendar, showing the movement of the herds of game animals, or else the phases of the moon which may then have helped to determine when certain animals were to be ritually killed.

Hunting weapons
The chief weapons of the Magdalenian hunters were the spear and harpoon. To throw these even further they used a spear-thrower. Spearheads and harpoons were hafted onto long wooden shafts, the bases of which fitted into grooves in the throwers. As the hunter hurled the spear he flicked his wrist, giving the weapon an extra push with the spear-thrower.
1 Ivory and horn spearheads.
2 Barbed harpoons.

Spear-throwers
3 How Magdalenian hunters may have attached wooden shafts to their harpoons.
4 Spear-throwers were often very beautifully carved: A this one has a figure of a roe deer on it; B a grouse; C two views of a spear-thrower carved with an ibex.
5 How spear-throwers were used. A leather thong attached the thrower to the huntsman's wrist. Spear-throwers have been used by hunters throughout the world for thousands of years.

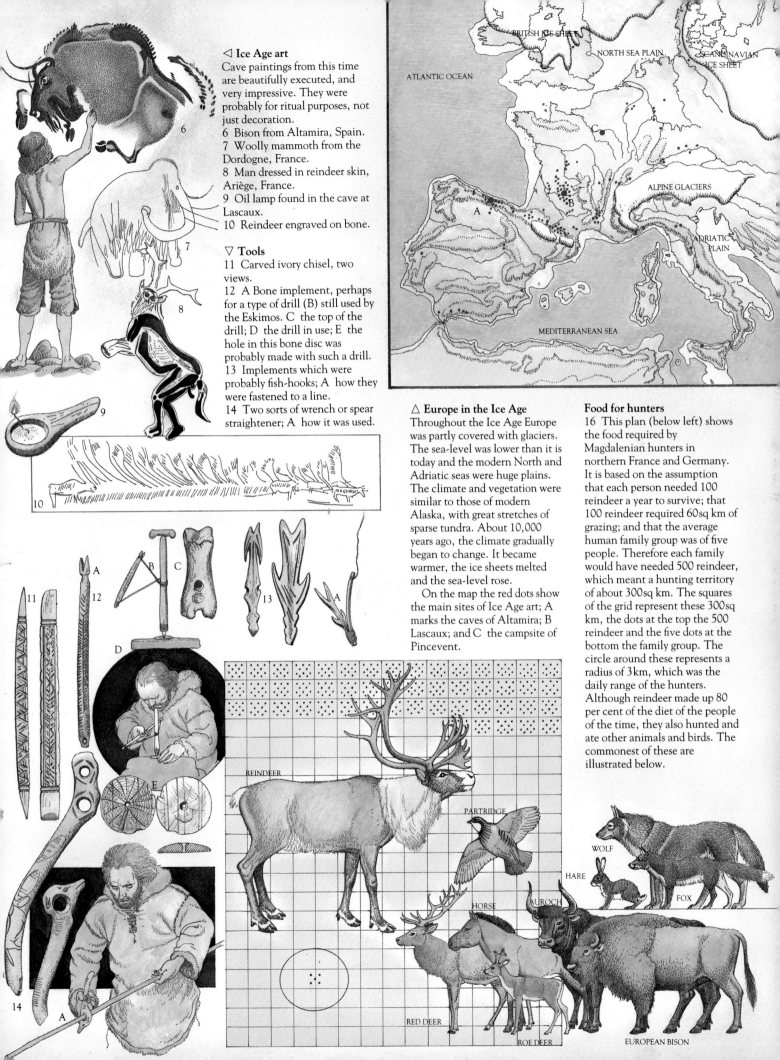

◁ Ice Age art
Cave paintings from this time are beautifully executed, and very impressive. They were probably for ritual purposes, not just decoration.
6 Bison from Altamira, Spain.
7 Woolly mammoth from the Dordogne, France.
8 Man dressed in reindeer skin, Ariège, France.
9 Oil lamp found in the cave at Lascaux.
10 Reindeer engraved on bone.

▽ Tools
11 Carved ivory chisel, two views.
12 A Bone implement, perhaps for a type of drill (B) still used by the Eskimos. C the top of the drill; D the drill in use; E the hole in this bone disc was probably made with such a drill.
13 Implements which were probably fish-hooks; A how they were fastened to a line.
14 Two sorts of wrench or spear straightener; A how it was used.

△ Europe in the Ice Age
Throughout the Ice Age Europe was partly covered with glaciers. The sea-level was lower than it is today and the modern North and Adriatic seas were huge plains. The climate and vegetation were similar to those of modern Alaska, with great stretches of sparse tundra. About 10,000 years ago, the climate gradually began to change. It became warmer, the ice sheets melted and the sea-level rose.

On the map the red dots show the main sites of Ice Age art; A marks the caves of Altamira; B Lascaux; and C the campsite of Pincevent.

Food for hunters
16 This plan (below left) shows the food required by Magdalenian hunters in northern France and Germany. It is based on the assumption that each person needed 100 reindeer a year to survive; that 100 reindeer required 60 sq km of grazing; and that the average human family group was of five people. Therefore each family would have needed 500 reindeer, which meant a hunting territory of about 300 sq km. The squares of the grid represent these 300 sq km, the dots at the top the 500 reindeer and the five dots at the bottom the family group. The circle around these represents a radius of 3 km, which was the daily range of the hunters. Although reindeer made up 80 per cent of the diet of the people of the time, they also hunted and ate other animals and birds. The commonest of these are illustrated below.

The fisher~hunters

The Mesolithic, or Middle Stone Age, period, which followed the Palaeolithic Age, marks a turning point in prehistoric culture. The climate changed dramatically and intensive hunting caused the extinction of the large herds of animals which had grazed over northern Europe throughout the Palaeolithic period. Between 13,000 and 8,000 years ago the mammoth, bison and other large animals became extinct, and only reindeer remained in the far north to provide food for the tribes of hunters.

A different climate
During this time the climate gradually became warmer. This change, of course, affected everything else. The higher temperatures melted the ice cap which had covered large areas of Europe for many thousands of years. Although this made the sea-level rise and the landmass diminish, it also meant that humans and animals could now live on land which had previously been covered with ice.

In the milder wetter climate forests grew where before there had been poor, barren tundra. As a result, increasing numbers of different birds and animals colonised the woods and forests.

A changing lifestyle
Mesolithic peoples had to adapt to these changes of climate, vegetation and animal life. They built their settlements near water, either freshwater rivers and lakes or saltwater lagoons and estuaries, because such places provided a wide variety of food. Plants were the main source of food, but there is plenty of evidence from Mesolithic campsites to show that fish, shellfish, birds and mammals were also eaten.

New tools are invented
Stone tools also changed dramatically at this time – from large hand-axes to tiny flint blades a few centimetres long. These tiny blades were fixed into bone, antler, or wooden implements to give a good cutting edge. This increased the different types of tool and also meant that if a blade became blunt or broken it could be replaced, without having to make a whole new tool. The bow and arrow also came into use, and revolutionized hunting.

The number of fish-traps, nets, harpoons and hooks found by archaeologists show the importance of fish and seafood in people's diet. Lepenski Vir, on the Danube in Yugoslavia, is a good example of a village economy based on fishing. Shell middens – enormous heaps of shells – by sites on the Atlantic show how much shellfish Mesolithic peoples ate if it was available.

△ **Mesolithic homes**
Tents covered with animals skins were probably the most usual type of home for Mesolithic peoples in northern Europe. Evidence found at many sites, from Ireland to Denmark, suggests that the tents were round, rather like those of modern Lapps.

Styles of clothing
1 These female figures were painted on a rock at Cogul, Spain.
2 Reconstruction, based on 1, of what a woman in Mesolithic Europe may have worn. The basket, although dating from later prehistoric times, may have been used earlier.
3 Hunter with a bow and arrow, painted at Gasuna Gorge, Spain.
4 A group of hunters from Cueva de Val del Characo del Agua Amarga; B hunter from El Secans, both in Spain.
5 Reconstructed hunting scene based on the rock paintings from Spain. The leather shorts, head-dress with feathers and belt hung with animal tails are all suggested in the paintings. Also with these hunters is a dog. This period saw the first evidence that dogs were being domesticated.

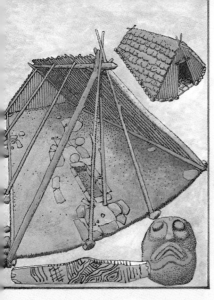

▷ **Europe after the glaciers melted**

This map shows Europe at the beginning of the Mesolithic period. Although the sea-level had risen, there was still quite a large plain joining Britain and Europe.

The red dots show the principal Mesolithic sites: 1 Star Carr, 2 Klosterlund, 3 Ofnet, 4 Tardenois, 5 the area of rock painting in eastern Spain, 6 Lepenski Vir, 7 Mas d'Azil, 8 Arene Candide.

△ **A settled community**

Some Mesolithic peoples lived in villages and did not follow a nomadic hunting existence. One such village was at Lepenski Vir, near the Iron Gates gorge of the Danube in Yugoslavia. Here the people built large houses with paved floors and large hearths, over which they probably smoked fish from the Danube. The people of Lepenski Vir also made the first sculpture known in Europe. One of these is shown in the picture together with a carved stone slab which may have been used to kill fish taken from the fish traps.

Mesolithic weapons

6 Elm bow, Denmark.

7-9 Small flint flakes were struck from large cores. The flakes were put in a wooden grip (A) and worked with another tool to give them a sharp edge.

10 A-G different ways in which large blades were broken and used for other tools.

11-15 Types of arrowhead.

16-17 Blunt arrows used for shooting birds and small game.

18-20 Modern Eskimo arrows used for the same purposes as 16 and 17.

21 Transverse arrowhead for shooting birds (the wing was broken by the blade), Denmark.

22 Group of microliths, tiny flint blades, from North Africa.

23-25 Remains of Mesolithic arrows.

26 Flint dagger with leather sheath and belt.

Mesolithic hunters

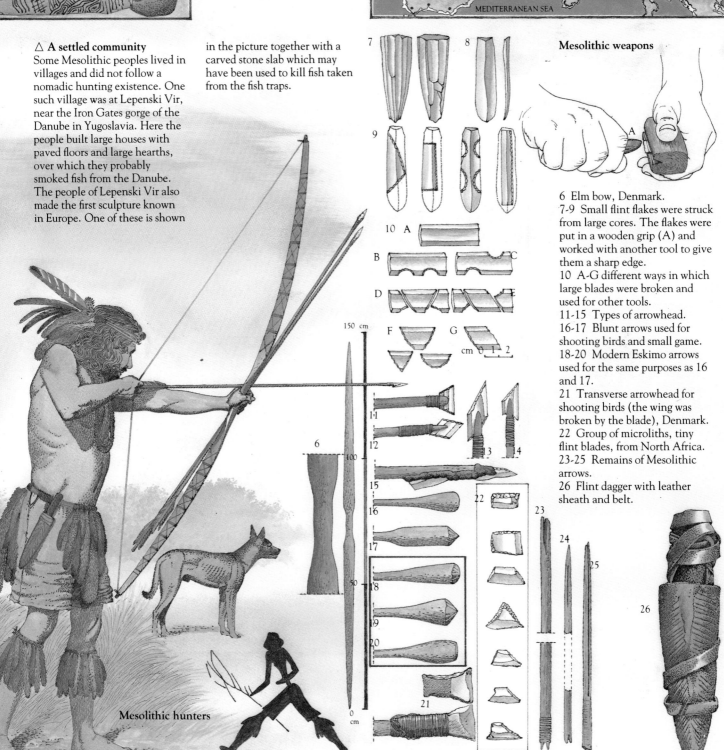

A fine Mesolithic site

Star Carr in Yorkshire, England is one of the best and most closely studied of Mesolithic sites in Europe. The settlement was beside a lake in what is now the valley of the River Derwent. The village probably consisted of a few tents made of skin, each one resting on a platform of birchwood. It dates to 9,500 years ago and was probably very like other Mesolithic villages which were dotted about on the huge plain, now covered by the North Sea, which stretched from Britain to Denmark.

Life at Star Carr

Archaeologists believe that about four families lived in the village, exploiting an area around the camp of between 30 and 100 square kilometres. Almost everything they needed (shown in the illustration opposite) was available within one hour's walk of the village. Indeed, scientists have described the people of this period as gatherer-hunter-fishers who skilfully exploited their environment without ever endangering the plants and animals on which they depended for food and clothing.

The village was only used during the winter, which suggests that the families who lived there followed the seasonal movement of the animals they hunted. Red deer still live on the hills around Star Carr, and the families from there may have followed the herds of these deer, which were much larger in Mesolithic times than they are today.

These early settlers may even actually have herded the deer, as a reliable source of fresh meat and other necessities, and driven them to fresh pastures with the changing of the seasons.

Clothing in Mesolithic times

It is always difficult to know what people living so long ago wore. From their skeletons we know that Mesolithic people were tall and muscular. Tools and weapons survive so we know how they hunted and fought. But clothes, being made of softer materials, seldom remain.

As the climate became milder, so clothing probably became lighter. Thick furs and skins were no longer essential for survival, and regional variations in dress may well have developed.

Art and culture

The warmer climate and good food supplies made life much easier. As a result art and culture slowly began to develop. In Spain, for example, paintings on the walls of caves and rock shelters show hunting scenes and, for the first time in human history, scenes of warfare. From the evidence left by these artists, the bow and arrow was the most common weapon both for hunting and for war.

Mesolithic fishermen
1 Fish trap made of osiers, Denmark. Traps like this are still used for catching salmon in Sweden.
2 Fragment of an oar, Star Carr.
3 Flint adze in a wooden holder which was fixed on a wooden handle and used to make dug-out canoes.

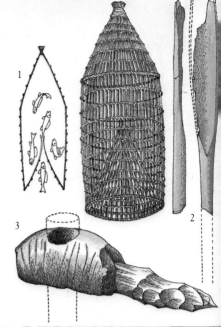

▽ **Reconstruction of a fishing scene** near a Mesolithic campsite. There are many Mesolithic sites near rivers, streams and lakes, because in such places there was always a good food supply: fish, shellfish, water birds and other birds and animals which came to the water to drink. Bows were used to shoot harpoons at fish as well as to fire arrows at other game.

4-6 Barbed harpoons made from antler horn.
7-8 Methods of hafting harpoons.
9 Bone fishhooks; A how bait was attached to the hooks.
10 Making a shellfish hook.
11 Barbed harpoons made from many small flint blades.
12 Harpoons of the French Azilian culture were better than many earlier ones. The early ones could pull out of the animal if the shaft came away from the harpoon itself (A-C). The curved Azilian ones swivelled and stuck (D-E).

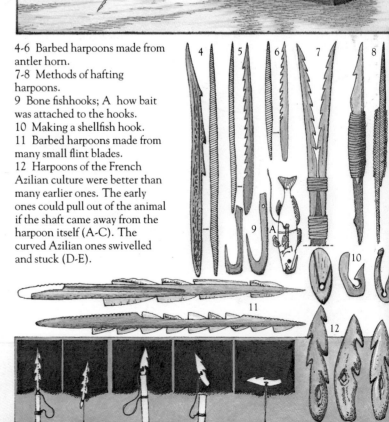

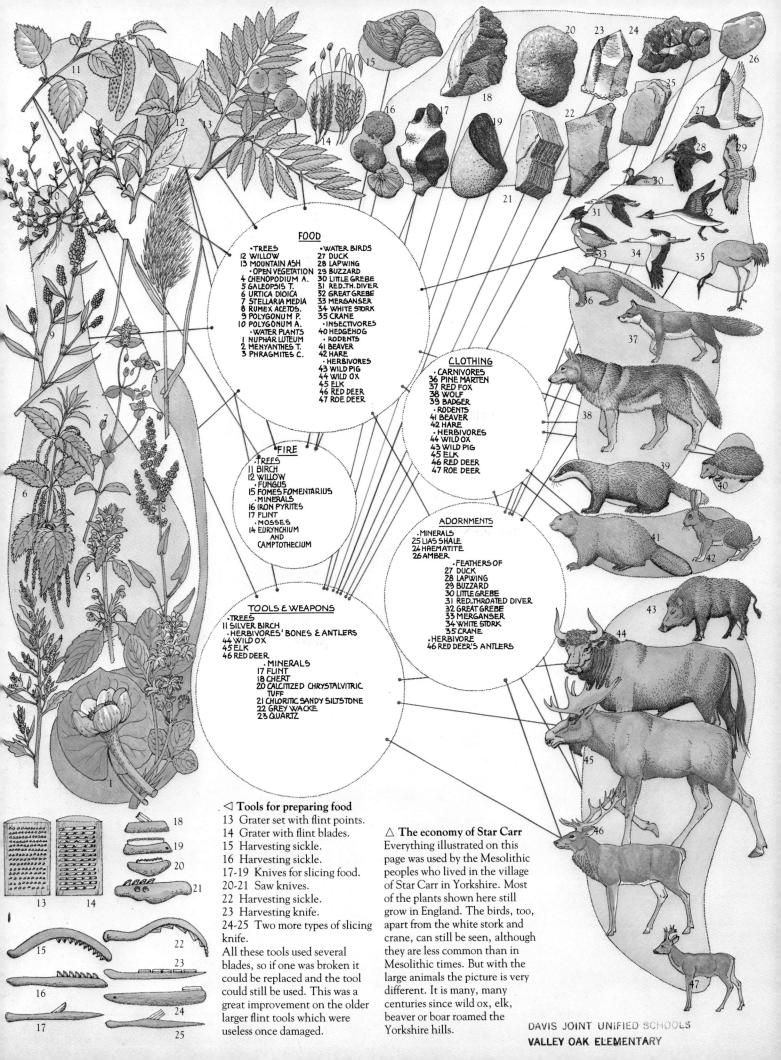

FOOD

- TREES
  - 12 WILLOW
  - 13 MOUNTAIN ASH
- OPEN VEGETATION
  - 4 CHENOPODIUM A.
  - 5 GALEOPSIS T.
  - 6 URTICA DIOICA
  - 7 STELLARIA MEDIA
  - 8 RUMEX ACETOS.
  - 9 POLYGONUM P.
  - 10 POLYGONUM A.
- WATER PLANTS
  - 1 NUPHAR LUTEUM
  - 2 MENYANTHES T.
  - 3 PHRAGMITES C.

- WATER BIRDS
  - 27 DUCK
  - 28 LAPWING
  - 29 BUZZARD
  - 30 LITTLE GREBE
  - 31 RED.TH. DIVER
  - 32 GREAT GREBE
  - 33 MERGANSER
  - 34 WHITE STORK
  - 35 CRANE
- INSECTIVORES
  - 40 HEDGEHOG
- RODENTS
  - 41 BEAVER
  - 42 HARE
- HERBIVORES
  - 43 WILD PIG
  - 44 WILD OX
  - 45 ELK
  - 46 RED DEER
  - 47 ROE DEER

FIRE

- TREES
  - 11 BIRCH
  - 12 WILLOW
- FUNGUS
  - 15 FOMES FOMENTARIUS
- MINERALS
  - 16 IRON PYRITES
  - 17 FLINT
- MOSSES
  - 14 EURYNCHIUM
    AND
    CAMPTOTHECIUM

CLOTHING

- CARNIVORES
  - 36 PINE MARTEN
  - 37 RED FOX
  - 38 WOLF
  - 39 BADGER
- RODENTS
  - 41 BEAVER
  - 42 HARE
- HERBIVORES
  - 44 WILD OX
  - 43 WILD PIG
  - 45 ELK
  - 46 RED DEER
  - 47 ROE DEER

ADORNMENTS

- MINERALS
  - 25 LIAS SHALE
  - 24 HAEMATITE
  - 26 AMBER
- FEATHERS OF
  - 27 DUCK
  - 28 LAPWING
  - 29 BUZZARD
  - 30 LITTLE GREBE
  - 31 RED.THROATED DIVER
  - 32 GREAT GREBE
  - 33 MERGANSER
  - 34 WHITE STORK
  - 35 CRANE
- HERBIVORE
  - 46 RED DEER'S ANTLERS

TOOLS & WEAPONS

- TREES
  - 11 SILVER BIRCH
- HERBIVORES' BONES & ANTLERS
  - 44 WILD OX
  - 45 ELK
  - 46 RED DEER
- MINERALS
  - 17 FLINT
  - 18 CHERT
  - 20 CALCITIZED CHRYSTALVITRIC TUFF
  - 21 CHLORITIC SANDY SILTSTONE
  - 22 GREY WACKE
  - 23 QUARTZ

◁ **Tools for preparing food**
13 Grater set with flint points.
14 Grater with flint blades.
15 Harvesting sickle.
16 Harvesting sickle.
17-19 Knives for slicing food.
20-21 Saw knives.
22 Harvesting sickle.
23 Harvesting knife.
24-25 Two more types of slicing knife.
All these tools used several blades, so if one was broken it could be replaced and the tool could still be used. This was a great improvement on the older larger flint tools which were useless once damaged.

△ **The economy of Star Carr**
Everything illustrated on this page was used by the Mesolithic peoples who lived in the village of Star Carr in Yorkshire. Most of the plants shown here still grow in England. The birds, too, apart from the white stork and crane, can still be seen, although they are less common than in Mesolithic times. But with the large animals the picture is very different. It is many, many centuries since wild ox, elk, beaver or boar roamed the Yorkshire hills.

Çatal Hüyük: the first city

For centuries it was thought that the Middle East was the cradle of civilization, and this seems to be confirmed by modern research. It was in the Middle East, for example, that men first left the roaming lifestyle of hunting and gathering and grouped themselves into urban societies. They began to build their homes of mud and reeds close to one another. The first settled communities grew up – probably one of the greatest changes ever to occur in the evolution of human society, and a forerunner of our lifestyle today.

An early city

One of the world's earliest cities was discovered at Çatal Hüyük, on the edge of the Konya plateau in south central Turkey, in the 1950s. Although only part of the site was excavated, twelve levels of building were uncovered. The oldest shows that a city flourished there in 6150 BC.

The brick houses were built on a rectangular plan, one beside the other, with no room for streets. Access to the houses was through openings in the roofs, and the inhabitants went about the town by walking across the roofs.

Each of the twelve building levels represents one city, because when one was destroyed the next was built on the rubble. In this way a hill was formed during the 800 years the site was inhabited.

As the buildings rose in terraces up the slope of the hill each was higher than the previous one, and windows were made in the vertical wall overlooking the roof of the house below. Rubbish and sanitation were dealt with out-of-doors in ruined houses or square courts.

Defending the city

Because the houses were built side by side, the outside of the city was a continuous wall with no openings of any kind. This meant that no further defences were necessary. Indeed, it would have been very hard to capture the city, because any invaders would have had to dislodge the defenders from one house at a time, while facing a hail of stones and arrows from the next. Perhaps this is why no sign of war has been found at Çatal Hüyük.

Feeding the city

Agriculture around Çatal Hüyük was extensive and efficient. Apart from cereals, such as barley and bread wheat, peas and vetches were also grown. Vegetable oils were made from plants and nuts. A type of beer may also have been produced. Although hunting was still quite important, sheep and cattle were kept for food and clothing.

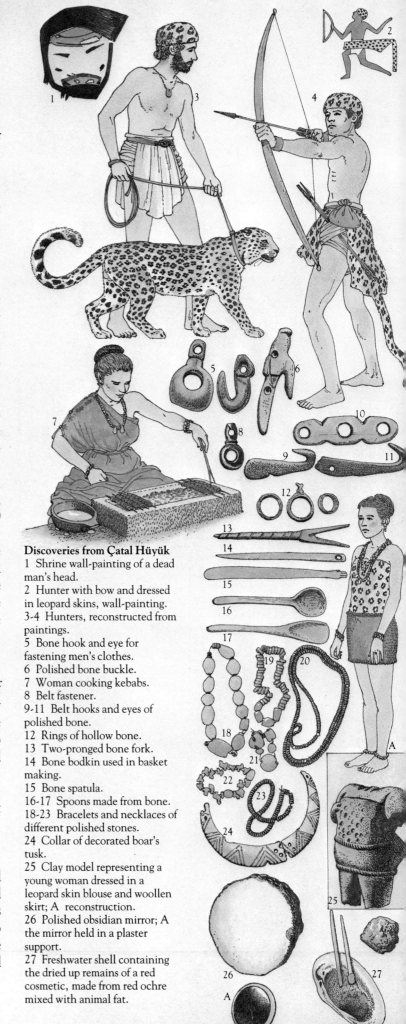

Discoveries from Çatal Hüyük
1 Shrine wall-painting of a dead man's head.
2 Hunter with bow and dressed in leopard skins, wall-painting.
3-4 Hunters, reconstructed from paintings.
5 Bone hook and eye for fastening men's clothes.
6 Polished bone buckle.
7 Woman cooking kebabs.
8 Belt fastener.
9-11 Belt hooks and eyes of polished bone.
12 Rings of hollow bone.
13 Two-pronged bone fork.
14 Bone bodkin used in basket making.
15 Bone spatula.
16-17 Spoons made from bone.
18-23 Bracelets and necklaces of different polished stones.
24 Collar of decorated boar's tusk.
25 Clay model representing a young woman dressed in a leopard skin blouse and woollen skirt; A reconstruction.
26 Polished obsidian mirror; A the mirror held in a plaster support.
27 Freshwater shell containing the dried up remains of a red cosmetic, made from red ochre mixed with animal fat.

The earliest city?

28 Artist's impression, based on the archaeological excavations of level VI, of how the town of Çatal Hüyük probably looked when it was inhabited about 6000 BC. Because of the way the houses were built one up against the other, the rooms were probably rather dark inside, the only light entering them through small windows set high up in the walls. There were little raised covers to the roof access hatches through which people entered or left the houses.

29 Wall-painting from a shrine which shows the town of Çatal Hüyük rising in terraces closely packed with rectangular houses. In the background is an erupting volcano, Hasan Dag, clearly visible from the site of Çatal Hüyük.

30 A brick-maker using a wooden frame to shape the bricks used in building the houses and shrines at Çatal Hüyük. The bricks were not fired in kilns, but dried in the sun.

31 Reconstruction of the typical main room in a house excavated in level VI at Çatal Hüyük. The arrangement of the interior depended entirely on the position of the windows, but the rooms were frequently rectangular.

▷ The origin of the city?
The dots on this map mark the sites of some of the most important and earliest cities mankind ever built. Although there were early cities in Egypt, it is interesting that there was a great concentration of city-building in the area covered by the map.

▷ The layout of Çatal Hüyük
Aerial plan of part of the city of Çatal Hüyük drawn up by archaeologists. Note the large number of shrines. Like the houses, the shrines were probably entered via the roof. The darkness, caused by the small windows high in the walls, must have added to the mystery of the ceremonies carried out in them.

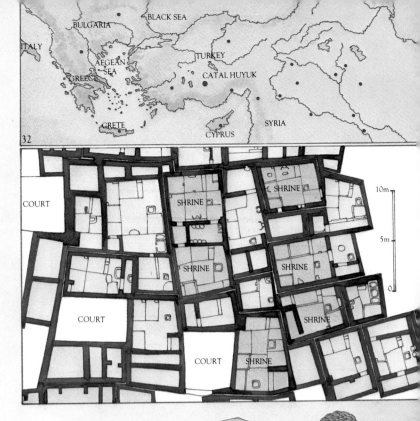

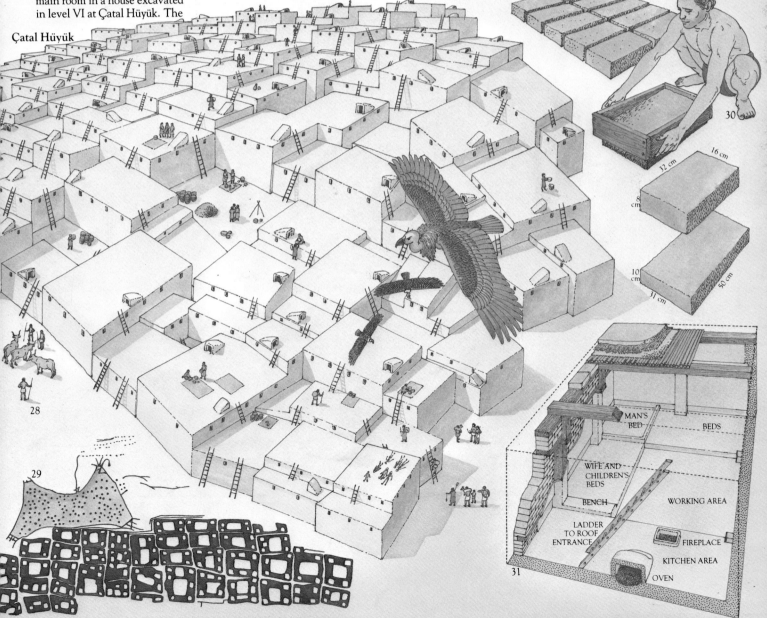

Çatal Hüyük

Cloth-making at Çatal Hüyük

1 Woman weaving at an upright mat loom.

2 Woman spinning wool into thread before weaving.

3 Spindle. No spindle whorl (the weight on the end of the spindle) has been found in the excavations, which suggests that the spindles used by these people were made entirely of wood.

4 The looms used at Çatal Hüyük may have been ground looms. The main yarn was wool, although camel and goat hair may also have been used.

6 HEDDLE ROD
SHED STICK
BREAST BEAM
WARP BEAM
A

7 SWORD-BEATER
COUNTER SHED
B

8

5 Textile design drawn from a wall-painting. It is a pattern still commonly found on modern Turkish rugs.

6-7 Diagrams showing how a ground loom works. A shows the position of the warp threads when the shed is formed and B when the counter-shed is formed. The position of the sword-beater which packs the threads of the 'weft' (the cross threads) together is also shown in B.

8 Baked clay seals are very common in the excavations of level VI at Çatal Hüyük. Although it has been suggested that such seals were used to stamp patterns on the body as a form of decoration, it is much more likely that they were used to stamp different coloured patterns on to cloth.

Shrines and sanctuaries

A remarkable feature of Çatal Hüyük is the number of buildings which appear to have been shrines or sanctuaries. Forty have been discovered scattered over nine of the excavated levels of the city.

Although the shrines are similar in structure to the houses, they are outstanding for their decoration and contents. They have plaster walls with fine paintings or reliefs showing bulls' heads, human figures and animals. The dead were buried beneath plaster platforms which may have been used as altars. The excavations suggest that the bodies of the dead were first left on the rooftops for the vultures to pick the bones. Then the skull was removed before the skeleton was wrapped up, put in a basket and buried.

In the shrines archaeologists have found small statues of clay or stone. These seem to represent the gods the city worshipped. Other statues showed bulls and rams. They were modelled in clay on a base of straw or wood. Frequently real skulls and horns were incorporated into the statues.

Many of the statues and reliefs were decorated with the same patterns and pigments used in the wall-paintings. Ochre, in various shades of brown, was the chief colour. It came from the hills near the city which also provided other pigments for making colours, such as cinnabar and iron ores which gave different types of red.

A centre of trade

Tools made of obsidian (a type of volcanic glass) have been found in large numbers at Çatal Hüyük. The obsidian probably came from the nearby volcanoes of Hasan Dag and Karaca Dag and archaeologists have found evidence to suggest that Çatal Hüyük was the centre of an extensive trade in it throughout western Anatolia (part of modern Turkey), Cyprus and the areas now called Israel, Lebanon and Syria. In return for the obsidian, the people of Çatal Hüyük received flint from Syria and seashells from the Mediterranean. The flint was useful for weapons, and the shells were used to make jewellery.

Other types of stone were also imported – archaeologists have found beads, grindstones and statues made of a type of stone not found in the area.

Skilled craftsmen

The flint and obsidian tools found at Çatal Hüyük are of a very high quality. Mirrors made of obsidian were polished so finely that even today there are no scratches on them. Weaving was also of a very high standard. The dry climate of the area has preserved some fragments of ancient cloth, and the quality is excellent.

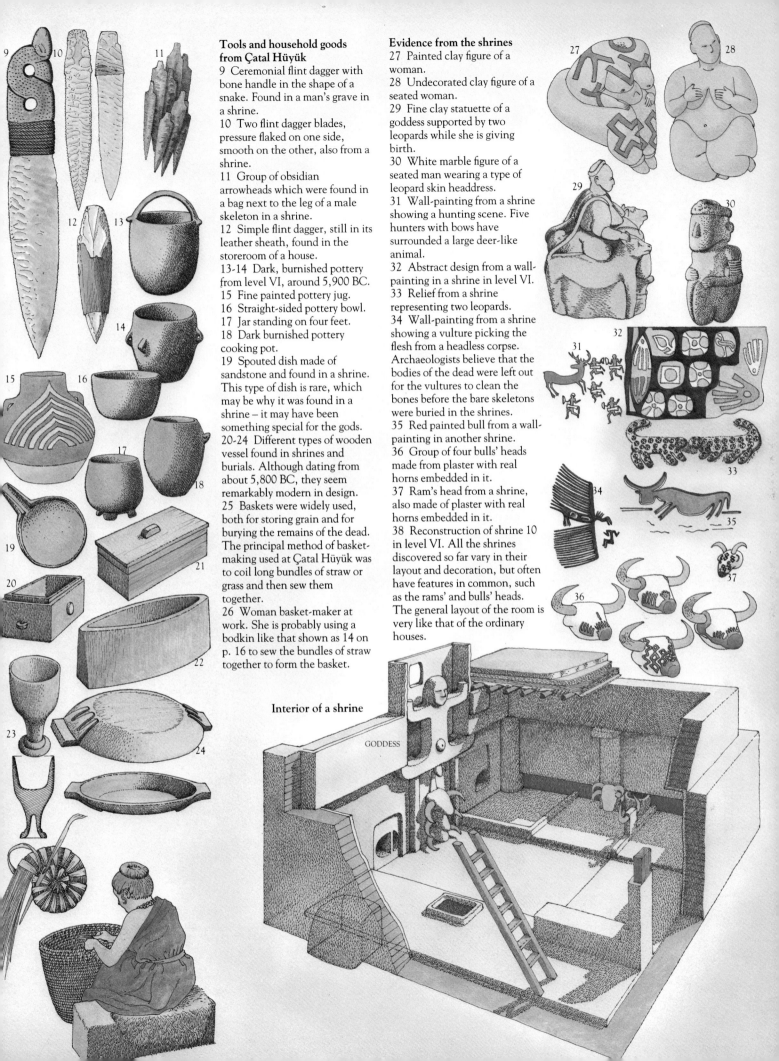

Tools and household goods from Çatal Hüyük

9 Ceremonial flint dagger with bone handle in the shape of a snake. Found in a man's grave in a shrine.

10 Two flint dagger blades, pressure flaked on one side, smooth on the other, also from a shrine.

11 Group of obsidian arrowheads which were found in a bag next to the leg of a male skeleton in a shrine.

12 Simple flint dagger, still in its leather sheath, found in the storeroom of a house.

13-14 Dark, burnished pottery from level VI, around 5,900 BC.

15 Fine painted pottery jug.

16 Straight-sided pottery bowl.

17 Jar standing on four feet.

18 Dark burnished pottery cooking pot.

19 Spouted dish made of sandstone and found in a shrine. This type of dish is rare, which may be why it was found in a shrine – it may have been something special for the gods.

20-24 Different types of wooden vessel found in shrines and burials. Although dating from about 5,800 BC, they seem remarkably modern in design.

25 Baskets were widely used, both for storing grain and for burying the remains of the dead. The principal method of basket-making used at Çatal Hüyük was to coil long bundles of straw or grass and then sew them together.

26 Woman basket-maker at work. She is probably using a bodkin like that shown as 14 on p. 16 to sew the bundles of straw together to form the basket.

Interior of a shrine

GODDESS

Evidence from the shrines

27 Painted clay figure of a woman.

28 Undecorated clay figure of a seated woman.

29 Fine clay statuette of a goddess supported by two leopards while she is giving birth.

30 White marble figure of a seated man wearing a type of leopard skin headdress.

31 Wall-painting from a shrine showing a hunting scene. Five hunters with bows have surrounded a large deer-like animal.

32 Abstract design from a wall-painting in a shrine in level VI.

33 Relief from a shrine representing two leopards.

34 Wall-painting from a shrine showing a vulture picking the flesh from a headless corpse. Archaeologists believe that the bodies of the dead were left out for the vultures to clean the bones before the bare skeletons were buried in the shrines.

35 Red painted bull from a wall-painting in another shrine.

36 Group of four bulls' heads made from plaster with real horns embedded in it.

37 Ram's head from a shrine, also made of plaster with real horns embedded in it.

38 Reconstruction of shrine 10 in level VI. All the shrines discovered so far vary in their layout and decoration, but often have features in common, such as the rams' and bulls' heads. The general layout of the room is very like that of the ordinary houses.

The first food producers

Farming and animal breeding began in the period known as the Neolithic or New Stone Age, which began about 6-8,000 years ago.

The domestication of wild animals and plants had begun thousands of years earlier. Primitive forms of animal herding had existed since Palaeolithic times, but usually it was man who followed the animals as they moved around in search of fresh grazing. During the Neolithic period this pattern changed.

The beginnings of agriculture

For the first time plants were grown deliberately for food. People no longer just gathered suitable plants that happened to be growing near their campsites. As a result communities became more settled – there is no point in planting crops if the group will move on before the crop can be harvested. Being able to grow enough food to eat brought great changes to society.

Because fodder crops were grown for animals, there was no need for them to move across the countryside seeking fresh grazing. They could now be kept in enclosures and fed, or allowed to graze freely in summer and then penned and fed during the winter months.

The first permanent villages

Growing crops and keeping animals in a restricted area allowed people to settle more permanently into villages. As a result larger, more substantial homes could be built. Instead of moving several times a year to follow the animals on which they depended, people now moved only every four or five years, when the soil of their fields was exhausted and crop yields were too poor to feed the villagers. The settlement was then abandoned, to be reoccupied years later when the fields had regained their fertility.

New crops appear

Farming settlements grew up in southeastern Europe, western Asia and the Middle East around 7-8,000 years ago. The ancestors of such modern crops as wheat and barley grew wild in the Middle East, where they were first cultivated. Seeds of these crops, together with domesticated sheep and goats, probably reached Europe from the Middle East via the great rivers such as the Danube. Although their navigation was often difficult, Neolithic people are known to have used boats on them.

The village of Karanovo

CARRYING WATER

BEATING FLAX

SPINNING

POTTERY MAKING

THRESHING CORN

An early farming community

1 Model of the village at Karanovo, Bulgaria, as it was about 6,000 BC.
2 Typical house from Karanovo. It was about 4 by 8 metres, with the wooden wall posts stuck in a thick wall of clay. The village was rebuilt several times with slightly different house plans (A-D).
3 Clay model of a house from Strelice, Czechoslovakia.
4 Model house from Kodza, Bulgaria. Both date from 4,000 years ago.
5 Bone spatula or spoon, from Azmak, Bulgaria.
6 Bone tool; its use is unknown.
7 Side and end views of three polished stone axe-heads, Azmak and Bikova, Bulgaria.
8 Antler sickle with flint blades; A how the blades were set into the sickle.
9 Clay loom weight, southeast Hungary.
10 Large clay lamp, Azmak.
11 Large painted clay vase, Banjata, Bulgaria.
12 Unpainted clay vase, Azmak.
13 Pottery figurine of a woman.
14 Pot decorated with a human face, Azmak.

Karanovo was a busy farming village, as the illustration below shows. The scene is based on archaeological evidence found at the village and knowledge gained from studying similar farming cultures in present-day Africa and India. (The activities shown did take place at Karanovo, the remains at the village prove that, but *how* they were carried out is more of a problem, and it is in this area that archaeologists seek help from similar existing cultures.)

Pot-making

Fine pottery has been found in the village and surrounding region. It was made by coiling long rolls of clay round and round on top of one another, for the potter's wheel had not yet been invented. The pottery was fired to harden it by putting it in a shallow hole, and covering it with wood which was then set alight. This method was not very efficient and many pots got broken or cracked so badly they could not be used. Slowly kilns were developed and pottery was fired in these.

THRESHING

BASKET MAKING

CARRYING CORN FROM THE FIELD

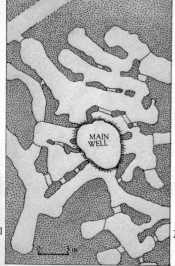

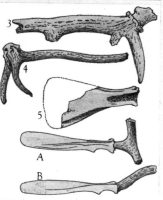

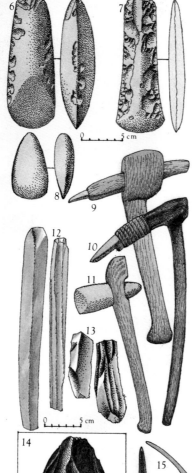

A new way of life

The new settled way of life which developed in Neolithic times undoubtedly caused immense changes in the structure of society. As a result of the more secure, regular food supplies, the population increased rapidly. Later, however, it stabilised, as the number of children surviving to adulthood kept pace with the number of people who died. The expanding farming communities gradually squeezed out the hunter-fishers as both competed for land.

New tools for a new lifestyle

Stone tools were still produced as they had been in Mesolithic times and large numbers of spear-points, arrowheads and knife-blades were made. However two new kinds of tools appeared – stone axes and adzes – which reflected the new way of life of the people of the time. These tools were used in woodworking which became more important than ever, because the settled communities needed strong, permanent houses. They were also important in the spread of agriculture, for forests had to be cleared and trees cut down to create fields for the crops.

The flint from which these tools were made was important in the economy of the time. It was mined in Britain and Belgium and exported over wide areas of northern Europe.

The development of crafts

People who live in settled communities have more time to make things like pottery than do people who are always moving from one place to another. So, although pottery, weaving and basket-making had been practised in earlier times, it was not until the Neolithic period that these skills really developed into fine craftsmanship.

Pottery, in particular, was very attractively designed. Kiln-fired pottery was made in many areas, and either engraved or painted with highly decorative patterns. Cloth-making and weaving, too, became more sophisticated, using techniques learned in basket-making. Although animal skins were still used, woven cloth was now more common for dressmaking.

Religion and ritual

Crafts are not the only aspect of culture to develop when people lead a settled way of life. Religion, and the rituals that go with it, play a much larger part in the lives of settled communities than they do for nomads. Although there is some evidence of burial accompanied by quite a lot of ritual from earlier times, there is a great deal more from this period. Because there was a relatively certain food supply, people had time to devote to things not directly connected with the everyday struggle for existence.

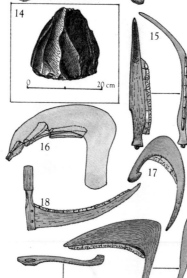

Flint mines and tools
Flint was important in the economy of Neolithic Europe. It was mined in various places in northwestern Europe and then traded all over the continent.
1 The flint mines at Grimes Graves, Norfolk, England, were very extensive. From a central well, galleries were excavated horizontally, following the flint strata.
2 The flint was got out of the ground with picks and rakes made of deer antlers.
3 Pick from Grimes Graves.
4 Rake found near Worthing, Sussex.
5 Shoulder blade shovel; A-B methods of hafting it.
6-8 Side and front views of three different types of stone axe.
9 Small axes were fixed into a wooden or antler holder before being hafted.
10 Tree roots made strong, flexible handles for axes.
11 Another method of hafting.
12 High quality flint blades.
13 Flint flakes.

▷ **Obsidian**
Obsidian, or volcanic 'glass', is found in southern and eastern Europe. Like flint, it was mined and traded in Neolithic times.
14 The largest known obsidian core.
15-20 Different types of sickle, all with obsidian blades.

▷ **The development of settled agricultural communities in Europe**
1 Original habitat of einkorn; 2 original habitat of emmer; 3 original habitat of wild barley; 4 farming communities before 6000 BC; 5 Balkan cultures (including Karanovo) 6000-5000 BC; 6 Danubian culture 5000-4000 BC; 7 Impressed Ware and other western Mediterranean cultures 6000-5000 BC; 8 western Neolithic and associated cultures 4000-3000 BC; 9 Funnel Rim pottery culture 4000-3000 BC; 10 Tripolye culture 4000-3000 BC; 11 Boian and associated cultures 4000-3000 BC.

▷ **The wild ancestors of modern wheat and barley.**

◁ **Developing craft skills**
The increasingly settled life of Neolithic peoples is reflected in the technological quality of their artefacts.
21-22 Bone combs, Balkans.
23 Ring pendants.
24-25 Shell necklaces.
26 *Spondylus gaederopus* shell widely used for ornaments.
27 Front and side view of scraper for working skins; A method of hafting it.
28 Antler comb for working skins.
29 Three examples of Neolithic basketwork.
30 Three types of fishing net, from Denmark and Switzerland.
31 Embroidery found in Switzerland; A the stitches.
32 Diagram of a bread oven.
33 Using a saddle quern to grind corn.
34 Looms like this were used from Neolithic times to the end of the Roman empire.
35 Reconstruction of a longhouse of the Danubian culture, Holland.
36 Reconstruction of a house excavated in Hungary.
37-39 Danubian pottery decorated with incised lines.
40 Fine painted vase, Yugoslavia.
41-42 Vases with applied and incised decoration, Yugoslavia.
43 Clay figurine of a woman.
44-45 Two pots of the type called 'clay flame'. This was the finest Neolithic pottery.
46 Cup with ox-head handle.
47 Square mouthed clay vase.
48-50 Clay models of furniture.
51 Model of man with basket.
52 Fine painted vase, Rumania.
53 Clay model of a pottery kiln.

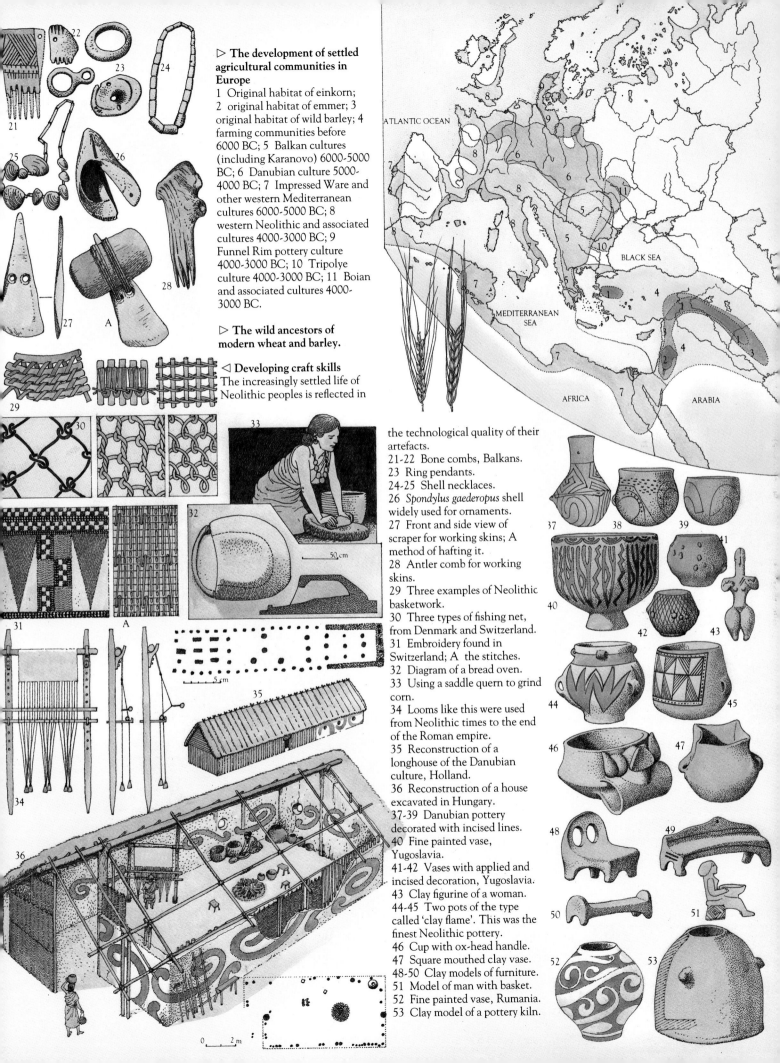

ATLANTIC OCEAN

MEDITERRANEAN SEA

BLACK SEA

AFRICA

ARABIA

The craftsmen of Egypt

The people of Ancient Egypt were one of the earliest civilizations in the world and have left more archaeological remains than any other ancient society. Thanks to the dry Egyptian climate, many of these have survived, providing evidence of daily life and also of the high standard of craftsmanship.

The River Nile and the 'Black Earth'
The narrow fertile strip of land each side of the River Nile was called the 'Black Earth' by the Ancient Egyptians. Now, as then, it stretches for about one thousand kilometres and is about 10 to 20 kilometres wide. On either side is the desert which was called the 'Red Earth'. The fertile Black Earth was formed by the great floods which take place each July and October. The floodwaters carry mud and silt which cover the fields and renew their fertility. It is not surprising that early men took advantage of this great richness and made the Nile valley a centre of agriculture from very early times.

The first Egyptian kingdoms
Around 3000 BC, the peoples living along the Nile valley formed into two kingdoms. Archaeologists call these the Upper and Lower Kingdoms. The former was around the Nile delta, while the latter was to the south. The two kingdoms were united in 2850 BC.

Historians divide the long centuries of Ancient Egyptian history into three periods. The first, known as the Old Kingdom, lasted from the unification of the kingdoms until c. 2181 BC. Then came the Middle Kingdom from c. 2052-c. 1786 BC (there was a short period of unrest between the two, but little is known about it).

At the end of the Middle Kingdom there was another period of troubles, but this time they were more serious. Peoples from the north, called the Hyksos, invaded Egypt and were not expelled until around 1570 BC. Then began the third period of Egyptian greatness – the New Kingdom, which lasted until about 1075 BC. After this Egypt suffered many invasions and her time of greatness was really over.

Government and taxation
The Egyptian state was headed by a king or 'pharaoh', who was worshipped as a god. The country was divided into districts, each one under the control of a local prince. He, together with various officials, was responsible for the good government of his area.

Domestic animals and crops from the fields were collected by the state as a form of tax, and the people also had to contribute their labour on a regular basis for the various building projects, such as the pyramids, undertaken by the pharaohs.

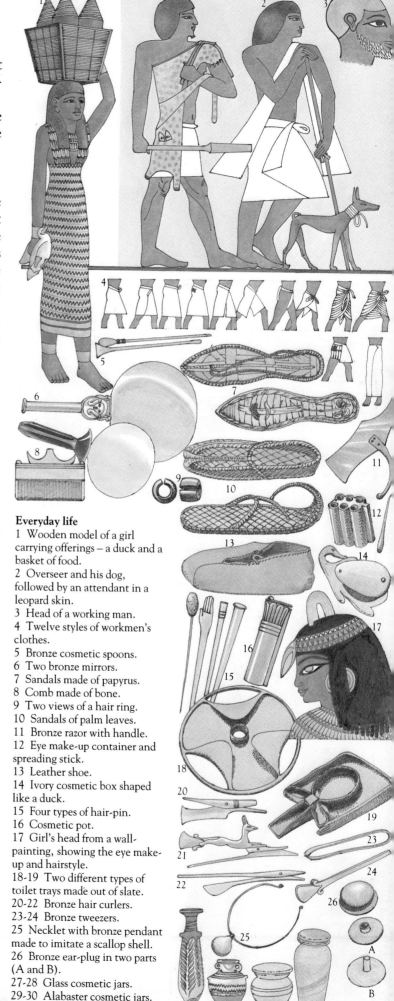

Everyday life
1 Wooden model of a girl carrying offerings – a duck and a basket of food.
2 Overseer and his dog, followed by an attendant in a leopard skin.
3 Head of a working man.
4 Twelve styles of workmen's clothes.
5 Bronze cosmetic spoons.
6 Two bronze mirrors.
7 Sandals made of papyrus.
8 Comb made of bone.
9 Two views of a hair ring.
10 Sandals of palm leaves.
11 Bronze razor with handle.
12 Eye make-up container and spreading stick.
13 Leather shoe.
14 Ivory cosmetic box shaped like a duck.
15 Four types of hair-pin.
16 Cosmetic pot.
17 Girl's head from a wall-painting, showing the eye make-up and hairstyle.
18-19 Two different types of toilet trays made out of slate.
20-22 Bronze hair curlers.
23-24 Bronze tweezers.
25 Necklet with bronze pendant made to imitate a scallop shell.
26 Bronze ear-plug in two parts (A and B).
27-28 Glass cosmetic jars.
29-30 Alabaster cosmetic jars.

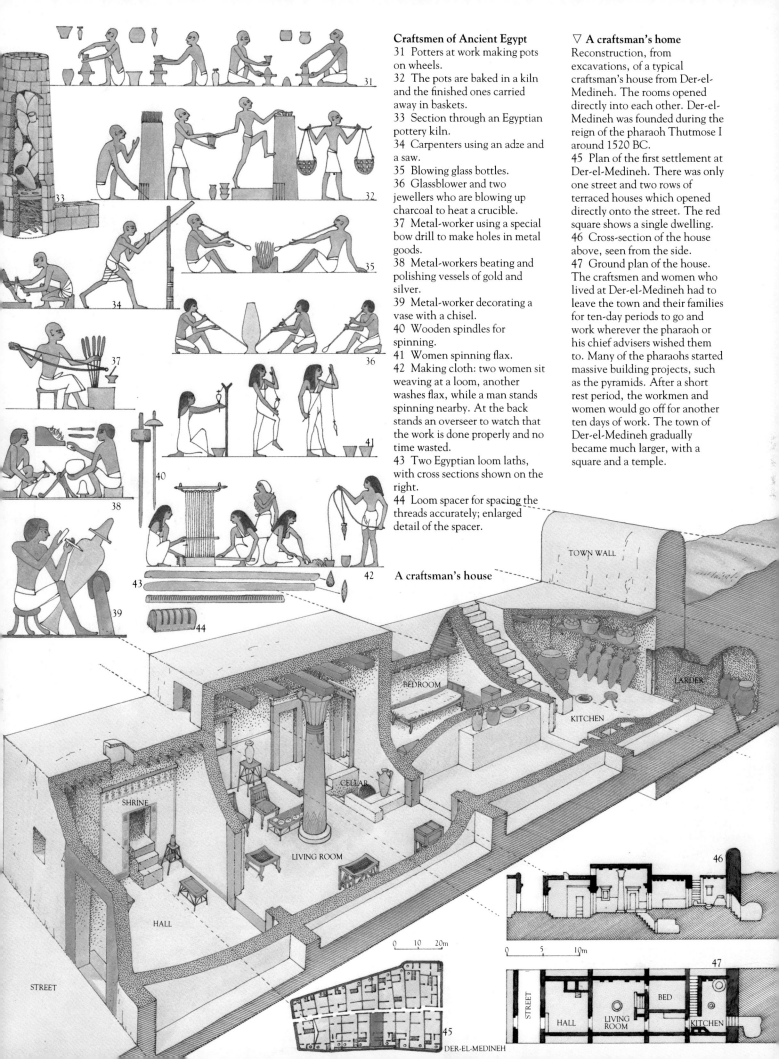

Craftsmen of Ancient Egypt
31 Potters at work making pots on wheels.
32 The pots are baked in a kiln and the finished ones carried away in baskets.
33 Section through an Egyptian pottery kiln.
34 Carpenters using an adze and a saw.
35 Blowing glass bottles.
36 Glassblower and two jewellers who are blowing up charcoal to heat a crucible.
37 Metal-worker using a special bow drill to make holes in metal goods.
38 Metal-workers beating and polishing vessels of gold and silver.
39 Metal-worker decorating a vase with a chisel.
40 Wooden spindles for spinning.
41 Women spinning flax.
42 Making cloth: two women sit weaving at a loom, another washes flax, while a man stands spinning nearby. At the back stands an overseer to watch that the work is done properly and no time wasted.
43 Two Egyptian loom laths, with cross sections shown on the right.
44 Loom spacer for spacing the threads accurately; enlarged detail of the spacer.

▽ **A craftsman's home**
Reconstruction, from excavations, of a typical craftsman's house from Der-el-Medineh. The rooms opened directly into each other. Der-el-Medineh was founded during the reign of the pharaoh Thutmose I around 1520 BC.
45 Plan of the first settlement at Der-el-Medineh. There was only one street and two rows of terraced houses which opened directly onto the street. The red square shows a single dwelling.
46 Cross-section of the house above, seen from the side.
47 Ground plan of the house. The craftsmen and women who lived at Der-el-Medineh had to leave the town and their families for ten-day periods to go and work wherever the pharaoh or his chief advisers wished them to. Many of the pharaohs started massive building projects, such as the pyramids. After a short rest period, the workmen and women would go off for another ten days of work. The town of Der-el-Medineh gradually became much larger, with a square and a temple.

A craftsman's house

TOWN WALL

BEDROOM

LARDER

KITCHEN

CELLAR

SHRINE

LIVING ROOM

HALL

STREET

46

0   10   20m

0   5   10m

47

STREET

HALL   LIVING ROOM   BED   KITCHEN

45
DER-EL-MEDINEH

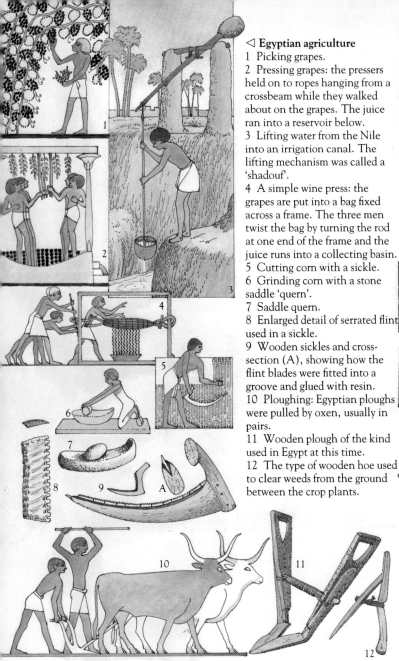

◁ Egyptian agriculture

1 Picking grapes.
2 Pressing grapes: the pressers held on to ropes hanging from a crossbeam while they walked about on the grapes. The juice ran into a reservoir below.
3 Lifting water from the Nile into an irrigation canal. The lifting mechanism was called a 'shadouf'.
4 A simple wine press: the grapes are put into a bag fixed across a frame. The three men twist the bag by turning the rod at one end of the frame and the juice runs into a collecting basin.
5 Cutting corn with a sickle.
6 Grinding corn with a stone saddle 'quern'.
7 Saddle quern.
8 Enlarged detail of serrated flint used in a sickle.
9 Wooden sickles and cross-section (A), showing how the flint blades were fitted into a groove and glued with resin.
10 Ploughing: Egyptian ploughs were pulled by oxen, usually in pairs.
11 Wooden plough of the kind used in Egypt at this time.
12 The type of wooden hoe used to clear weeds from the ground between the crop plants.

THE CRAFTSMEN OF EGYPT

Egyptian agriculture

Most Ancient Egyptians were involved in farming or in related industries such as wine-making, spinning or weaving. They had a well-developed system of irrigation, using water from the Nile channelled through canals and ditches to bring water to the fields.

Livestock rearing seems to have been efficient, and veterinary medicine was known. Papyrus scrolls tell of various cures and treatments for sick animals.

The family at home

Egyptian houses were very simple, made of wood and sun-dried bricks. Only the rich had much furniture. The father wielded strict discipline over his children. Early marriages and large families were encouraged.

Diet consisted mostly of bread, lentils, onions, vegetables and dried fish. The rich, however, enjoyed fruit, meat and game for their meals – as is shown on many wall-paintings.

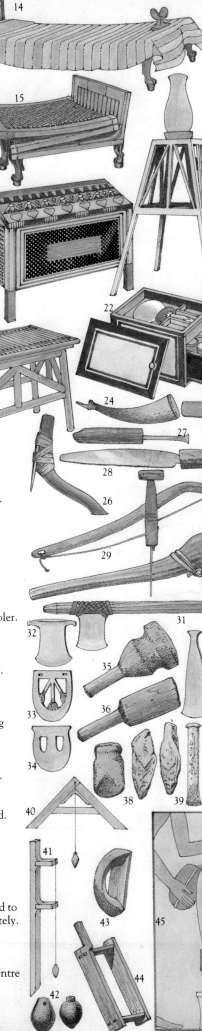

△ Domestic furniture

13 Commonest type of chair.
14 Bed with linen sheets.
15 Travelling bed.
16 Folding stool with legs shaped like ducks' heads.
17 Decorated wooden chest.
18 Lattice-work pot stand.
19 Wooden headrest. These were often used instead of pillows because they were cooler.
20 Stool with lattice legs.
21 Slatted-top table.
22 Decorated toilet casket.
23 Simple three-legged stool.

▷ Craftsmen's tools

24 Horn for oil.
25 Whetstone for sharpening tools, and an awl.
26 A carpenter's adze.
27 Chisel.
28 Saw with wooden handle.
29 Bow drill.
30 Another type of adze.
31 Axe with the blade hafted.
32-34 Axe heads.
35-36 Wooden mallets.
37 Adze heads.
38 Stone chisels.
39 Later iron chisels.
40 Square plumb level.
41 Vertical plumb level, used to cut blocks of masonry accurately.
42 Plumb line weights.
43 Plasterer's float.
44 Frame for making bricks.
45 Drill to hollow out the centre of stone containers.

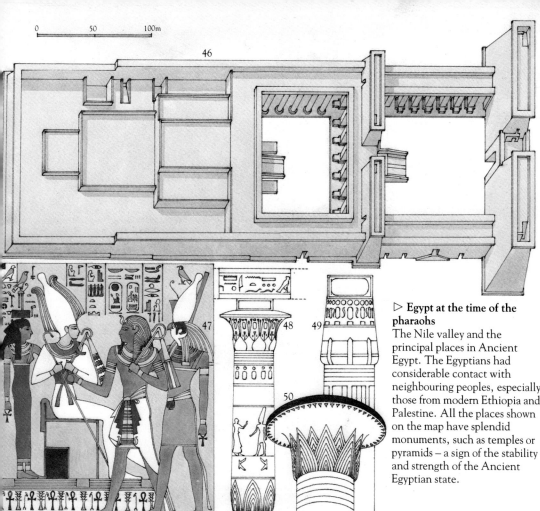

0   50   100m

46

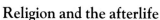

47 48 49

50

▷ **Egypt at the time of the pharaohs**
The Nile valley and the principal places in Ancient Egypt. The Egyptians had considerable contact with neighbouring peoples, especially those from modern Ethiopia and Palestine. All the places shown on the map have splendid monuments, such as temples or pyramids – a sign of the stability and strength of the Ancient Egyptian state.

MEDITERRANEAN SEA
ALEXANDRIA
LOWER EGYPT
EL GIZA
MEMPHIS
SAQQARA
PALESTINE
SINAI PENINSULA
MT SINAI
EL AMARNA
RED SEA
ARABIAN DESERT
THEBES
DER-EL-MEDINEH
KARNAK
LUXOR
ASWAN
UPPER EGYPT
0   100Km
NILE
ABU SIMBEL
ETHIOPIA

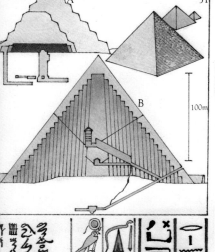

A   51
B
100m

△ **Egyptian architecture**
46 Aerial view of the sanctuary built by Ramses III at Medinet Habu c. 1170 BC.
47 Wall-painting showing the pharaoh Seti I being presented to the gods Isis and Osiris.
48-50 Finely carved and decorated pillars from the temple of Karnak.
51 The Egyptian pyramids are among the most impressive of all monuments to the dead.
Diagram A shows how the early stepped pyramid at Saqqara (green) developed from the simple 'mastaba' tomb (red). The Egyptian pyramid reached its finest form in the great pyramid at Giza (B), with its many passages and chambers.

52 53 54 57

55 56

58

59

60 61

◁ **Egyptian writing**
52 Demotic script handwritten on papyrus with a reed pen.
53 Monumental hieroglyphs painted on the wall of a tomb.
54 Hieroglyphs.

◁ **Decorative ware**
55 Polished red bottle.
56 Vase carved from granite.
57 Jar from a tomb.
58 Alabaster carved vessel.
59-60 Red pottery containers.
61 Vase carved from semi-precious hardstone.

Religion and the afterlife

The Ancient Egyptians believed very firmly in a life after death. Indeed, if it were not for this, we would know much less about them, for most of our knowledge is based on the many tomb paintings showing scenes of everyday life.

There were many gods and goddesses, all of whom had to be served with various rituals and prayers. One of the most important rituals was to ensure that the Nile flooded every year, because without the rich, fertile silt brought by the floods, the people of Egypt would have faced starvation.

This emphasis on a yearly cycle gave Egyptian religion and culture a continuity not encountered in other early civilizations.

The Egyptians also built tombs, the greatest of which were the pyramids, the tombs of the pharaohs. These contained a vast array of the dead ruler's possessions: furniture, jewellery and precious objects, put there to ensure a comfortable existence for their owner in the afterlife.

Egyptian writing: the hieroglyphs

The Egyptians developed a form of writing called 'hieroglyphic'. It consisted of symbols for words, consonants and groups of consonants; there were no signs for the vowels. This type of writing was usually sculpted or painted on monuments. A simplified form was used when writing with pen and ink on paper made from the papyrus reed.

Minoan Crete

On most of the Mediterranean islands, Neolithic farming peoples had been established for thousands of years. The early farmers in Crete grew crops such as olives, vines and cereals. By about 2500 BC their farming was so efficient and they achieved such good crops, that the plentiful supply of food allowed many people to do things other than work in the fields.

A developing civilization
Thanks to the good food supplies, a complex civilization quickly appeared. Towns were built on the eastern part of the island, each dominated by a vast palace which also acted as a sanctuary and a storehouse. Great quantities of oil, wine and grain were stored in these palaces, which were also centres of art and manufacture, as well as of justice.

Cretan society
Archaeologists do not know if the Cretan rulers were kings, priests, or considered gods (as was the case in Ancient Egypt). They do, however, know that Cretan society had many social classes and that it was an extremely efficient and self-confident society. The high standard of its architecture, arts and crafts suggest that many people were involved in these activities, with an equally large class of priests and nobles requiring luxury goods.

Knossos – the palace of the king
Much of our knowledge of Crete at this time comes from the great palace of Knossos. This was the home of the powerful King Minos who gave his name – Minoan – to the Cretan civilization of this time. Wonderfully preserved wall-paintings show how the people of this wealthy, successful civilization lived, the clothes they wore and the entertainments they enjoyed.

Trade
From their strategic position in the eastern Mediterranean, the Cretans traded widely, in particular with mainland Greece, Egypt and Syria. Their sea craft was unchallenged, and they bought back to the island the ivory and minerals they lacked.

Writing
Very early in their history, the people of Crete had developed a type of writing using little pictures and symbols to express their ideas. Around 1500 BC this had been replaced by two types of writing that archaeologists call 'Linear A' and 'Linear B'. Although the two forms of writing are related, only Linear B has been deciphered. Linear A remains a mystery, keeping still the secrets of the people who wrote it some 3,500 years ago.

Minoan dress and ornaments
1 A painted wall relief in the palace of Knossos shows a standing youth wearing the clothes and elaborate headdress of a young man from the upper class of Minoan society.
2 The clothes of Minoan women at the palace, showing the typical boleros and long skirts. Reconstructed from wall-paintings.
3 Painting on a coffin showing a religious ceremony performed by two women in front of an altar with the symbol of the double axe and the ' horns of consecration'.
4 Clay model.
5 Silver hairpin.
6 Earring made of gold.
7 Gold finger-ring.
8 Gold armlet.
9 Two views of a gold fish pendant.
10-11 Models of two goddesses showing the clothes worn by high-born ladies, queens or priestesses.
12 Gold earring.
13 Beads made of gold.
14 Decorative gold plaque.
15 Crouching lion ornament in gold.
16 A different type of gold plaque with decorative patterns in relief.
17 The type of clothes worn by women on the island of Thera, north of Crete.

The palace of Knossos

BLACK SEA
ITALY
MACEDONIA
GREECE
CRETE
CYPRUS
PHOENICIA
MEDITERRANEAN SEA
LIBYA
EGYPT

CRETE
KNOSSOS
ZAKROS

△ The palace of Knossos

18 Reconstruction of the palace at Knossos from the southern entrance.
19 Decorated column from the queen's bathroom.
20 Typical Minoan column.
21 Wall-painting showing a partridge and a hoopoe, both common birds around Knossos.
22 Fine decorative ceiling.
23 Stone lamps shaped like pillars were used to light the palace. The light was provided by a wick floating in animal fat.
24 Painted wall relief of a bull's head.
25 Painted plaster relief showing two griffins tied to a pillar.
26 Terracotta pipes were used for the drainage and water supply. They fitted one inside the other and were tied together by ropes passed through the small lugs along the sides of the pipes.

The palace of Zakros

27 The palace of Zakros was built on the extreme east coast of Crete. The plan shows the layout typical of Minoan palaces.

Crete and the Mediterranean

28 The map shows the position of Crete in relation to the other important cultures of the eastern Mediterranean.
29 Map showing where the great Minoan palaces were built on Crete.

▷ The work of Minoan craftsmen

30 The so-called 'throne of Minos', discovered at Knossos.
31 Stone table from Knossos.
32 Terracotta model of a carrying chair found at Knossos.
33 The bathtub used by the queen in the palace at Knossos.
34 Ritual vessel, shaped like a shell but made of alabaster.
35 Ritual vessel shaped like a bull's head and made from a semi-precious stone with wooden horns.
36 Vessel decorated with boxers.
37 Rock crystal and gold ritual vessel from Zakros.
38 Vessel decorated with a relief of a sanctuary, from Zakros.
39 'The chieftain's cup' from Agia Triada.

OLD PALACE

APARTMENTS OF THE FIRST PALACE PHASE

DINING ROOM

BATHROOM

STORE ROOM

LOBBY

DRAINS

WORK SHOPS

QUEEN'S

SHRINE

HALL OF CEREMONIES

CENTRAL COURT

APARTMENTS KING'S

CISTERN

BANQUET HALL

N

27

WORKSHOPS

The palace of Zakros

0   10   20m

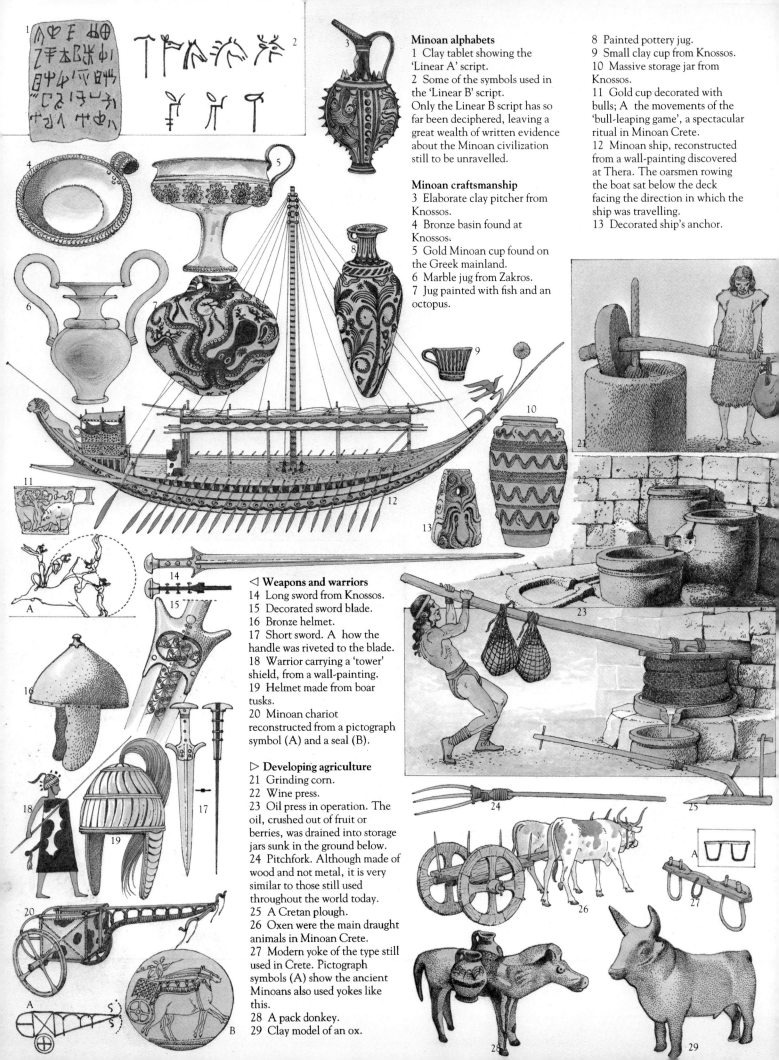

Minoan alphabets

1 Clay tablet showing the 'Linear A' script.

2 Some of the symbols used in the 'Linear B' script. Only the Linear B script has so far been deciphered, leaving a great wealth of written evidence about the Minoan civilization still to be unravelled.

Minoan craftsmanship

3 Elaborate clay pitcher from Knossos.

4 Bronze basin found at Knossos.

5 Gold Minoan cup found on the Greek mainland.

6 Marble jug from Zakros.

7 Jug painted with fish and an octopus.

8 Painted pottery jug.

9 Small clay cup from Knossos.

10 Massive storage jar from Knossos.

11 Gold cup decorated with bulls; A the movements of the 'bull-leaping game', a spectacular ritual in Minoan Crete.

12 Minoan ship, reconstructed from a wall-painting discovered at Thera. The oarsmen rowing the boat sat below the deck facing the direction in which the ship was travelling.

13 Decorated ship's anchor.

◁ **Weapons and warriors**

14 Long sword from Knossos.

15 Decorated sword blade.

16 Bronze helmet.

17 Short sword. A how the handle was riveted to the blade.

18 Warrior carrying a 'tower' shield, from a wall-painting.

19 Helmet made from boar tusks.

20 Minoan chariot reconstructed from a pictograph symbol (A) and a seal (B).

▷ **Developing agriculture**

21 Grinding corn.

22 Wine press.

23 Oil press in operation. The oil, crushed out of fruit or berries, was drained into storage jars sunk in the ground below.

24 Pitchfork. Although made of wood and not metal, it is very similar to those still used throughout the world today.

25 A Cretan plough.

26 Oxen were the main draught animals in Minoan Crete.

27 Modern yoke of the type still used in Crete. Pictograph symbols (A) show the ancient Minoans also used yokes like this.

28 A pack donkey.

29 Clay model of an ox.

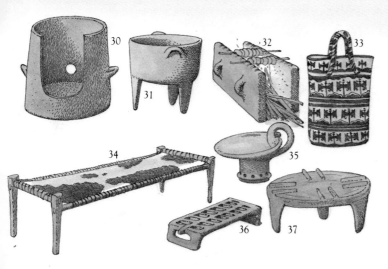

Destruction of a civilization

The ancient Minoan civilization was a peaceful one, engaged mainly in trade and the manufacture of fine goods which were eagerly sought by other Mediterranean peoples. Its end was, by contrast, violent. It would seem that a volcanic eruption on the small island of Thera, 70 miles north of Crete, had a traumatic effect on all the civilizations around the eastern Mediterranean. The eruption probably occurred about 1500 BC and certainly from this time onwards the civilization on Crete seems to have declined. Ancient myths tell of starvation, unrest and a general breakdown of society.

Archaeologists believe that clouds of volcanic dust may have obscured the sun and affected the weather, and that the volcanic ash from the volcano settled on fields, destroying the crops. The food stored in the great palaces soon ran out. Faced by starvation even the most peaceful societies are likely to disintegrate.

Crete after the Minoans

The palace of Knossos seems to have survived the eruption on Thera, but the people who ruled Crete from it were now Myceneans – from Mycenae on mainland Greece. By 1450 BC they had successfully asserted their domination and almost all traces of the Minoans' great civilization had disappeared. Not until 1900, when the British archaeologist, Arthur Evans, began to excavate at Knossos, did the modern world realize just how splendid Minoan Crete had been.

△ **Minoan household goods**
30 Clay oven.
31 Clay cooking pot.
32 Special bricks for cooking kebabs.
33 Clay vase shaped rather like a shopping bag.
34 Bed, from Thera.
35 Incense burner or oil lamp.
36 Clay grill. Grills like these were placed over hot coals and the food put on them to cook.
37 Clay table from Knossos.

▽ **The town of Zakros**
An artist's impression of what the town of Zakros may have looked like.

The large building in the background is the palace, from which the city was governed and where much of its wealth was stored in the form of grain, oil and wine. Archaeologists know what the houses looked like from pottery models found during the excavations.

The town of Zakros

Reconstructing Zakros
△ Pottery models found in excavations at the site of Zakros suggest that the people liked decorating their houses. The rather odd striped effects may have been made by different coloured bricks or else because the bricks were painted in different colours.

▷ Section of the excavated area of Zakros. It is an area of small houses and workshops. Because the town was hilly, many of the streets were little more than long flights of steps. This made the transport of goods difficult. Wheeled waggons and carts could only travel along the wider streets along the slope of the hillside. Pack-animals, such as horses, mules and donkeys, were the main form of transport.

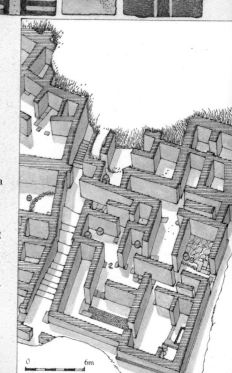

0   6m

People of the North

Prehistoric remains usually consist of stone tools and other artefacts of bone, pottery or metal. Perishable organic materials, such as wood, leather or cloth, are rarely found. It is even more rare for human corpses to be found, particularly when it is not just the skeletons that are preserved, but people still recognizable as people, with their skin, hair, flesh and clothes intact.

Such finds, however, have been made in northwestern Europe where, from the period known as the Bronze Age, many round burial mounds remain. In Denmark alone there were once perhaps as many as 50,000 burial mounds, almost all containing at least one body, and often several, and to this day they form one of the features of the Danish landscape. The people who created these mounds are known by archaeologists as the 'Mound People'.

The Mound People

The Mound People lived in Denmark over 3,000 years ago. When they died they were wrapped in an oxhide and buried in oak coffins along with their clothes, ornaments, tools, and weapons of bronze and gold. Over the coffins large monumental burial mounds were built.

The bodies are so well preserved because of the ground in which they were buried. It is damp and boggy, and the bog water, lacking oxygen and full of tannic acid from the oak coffins and other trees used to build the mounds, has acted as a preservative for all the buried organic materials – including human remains. This has given us a unique insight into their life.

Other Bronze Age burials

The round burial mounds found in Denmark were not the only type of burial used by European Bronze Age peoples. During the 15th and 14th centuries BC, people in eastern and central Europe cremated their dead and put the ashes in clay pots or 'urns', which were then buried in special cemeteries. Some of these cemeteries are large, containing up to a thousand burial urns. Archaeologists call such cemeteries 'urn fields'.

The earliest of the urn fields are in Hungary, Austria and eastern Germany, but later ones have also been found in Yugoslavia, the Netherlands and Spain.

Metal industries

Like the Mound Peoples' graves, the urn field burials often contain articles used by the dead people, including many fine ornaments and weapons. As the name 'Bronze Age' suggests, the chief metal used was bronze, although copper was also common at the beginning of the period. The standard of craftsmanship was extremely high.

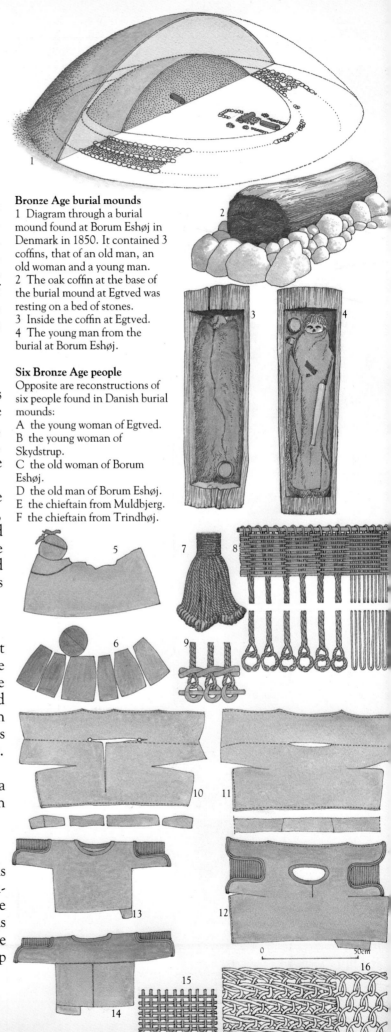

Bronze Age burial mounds
1 Diagram through a burial mound found at Borum Eshøj in Denmark in 1850. It contained 3 coffins, that of an old man, an old woman and a young man.
2 The oak coffin at the base of the burial mound at Egtved was resting on a bed of stones.
3 Inside the coffin at Egtved.
4 The young man from the burial at Borum Eshøj.

Six Bronze Age people
Opposite are reconstructions of six people found in Danish burial mounds:
A the young woman of Egtved.
B the young woman of Skydstrup.
C the old woman of Borum Eshøj.
D the old man of Borum Eshøj.
E the chieftain from Muldbjerg.
F the chieftain from Trindhøj.

Clothing details

5 The pattern of Trindhøj man's hat.
6 Another hat pattern.
7 Belt tassel.
8 The way in which the corded skirt found on the Egtved girl was made.
9 Detail of the edge of the Egtved skirt.
10 The pattern of the Egtved shirt.
11 The pattern of the shirt worn by the old woman found at Borum Eshøj.
12 Pattern for the shirt of the woman of Skydstrup.
13 Front view of the Skydstrup shirt.
14 Back of the Skydstrup shirt.
15 Enlarged detail of the fabric on the lower border of the shirt.
16 Detail of the embroidery around the neck opening of the Skydstrup shirt (enlarged).

Other contents of the graves

17 Birch bark container from the Egtved coffin. It contained a mixture of beer and apple wine when put into the coffin.
18 Small birch bark box from the Egtved coffin.
19 Ash wood folding stool with otter skin seat found in a coffin from Egtved.
20 Spiral rings of gold worn by Skydstrup woman in her hair.
21 Cup of ash wood decorated with bronze tacks, from Guldhøj.
22 Twisted bronze ring for wearing around the neck.
23 Bronze belt disk.
24 Decorative arm rings.
25 Pottery vessel.
26 Bronze fibula for fastening shirts.
27 Bronze button.
28 Small decorative disk.
29 Horn comb.
30 Spiral arm rings. (22-30 were all found on or in the grave of the old woman of Borum Eshøj.)
31 Leather purse with bronze fastener.
32 Fragment of a leather belt with bronze button.
33 Bronze razor wrapped in leather.
34 Bronze fibula. (31-34 were all found in the chief's coffin.)

35 Silver bracelet.
36-37 Sword and scabbard of the Muldbjerg chieftain.
38 Sword belonging to the Trindhøj chief.
39 Magic charms of wood wrapped in leather.
40 Sword, scabbard and belt of the Hvidegard chieftain.
41 Fragment of leather bag with buttoned belt.
42 Small bronze knife.
43 Dagger blade.
44 Bronze knife in its sheath.
45 Tweezers.
46 Birch bark box.
47 Bone comb.
48 Button.
49 Bronze fibula.
50-51 Knife blades.
52 Tweezers.
53 Button.
54 Small decorative disks.
55 Fibula.
56-57 Bronze disk and buttons.
58 Silver ring.
59 Needle.
60 Bead.
61 Button. (49-52 and 56-61 all belonged to the Trindhøj chief.)
62 A common type of shoe.

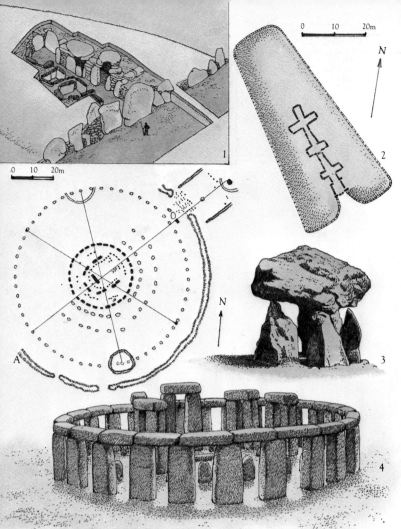

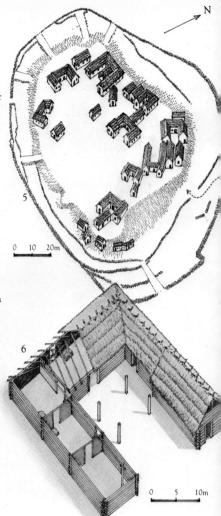

Bronze Age monuments

1 Diagram of the long barrow at West Kennett, Wiltshire, England showing the chambered tomb built about 5,000 years ago. The barrow was the cemetery for many generations of people from the area.

2 Aerial view of another long barrow, at Stony Littleton in Somerset. From this view it is easy to see why they are called 'long barrows'.

3 A 'dolmen' or 'table stone', was one of the simplest of burial chambers. A large capstone was supported by three or four smaller stones, giving the effect of a massive table. Many of these early monuments can still be seen in Brittany, France.

4 Stonehenge on Salisbury Plain in Wiltshire is probably the best-known of all European monuments from this time. The illustration shows it as it would have appeared to Bronze Age people. Many of the stones used in the making of Stonehenge were brought from places far away; A the layout of Stonehenge.

5 The Bronze Age settlement of Wasserburg in southern Germany, built about 1,000 BC.

6 Log hut from Wasserburg; the fireplaces are shown in red.

PEOPLE OF THE NORTH

Farming in Bronze Age Europe

Farming had improved enormously since the earlier Neolithic period. Although wild plants were still used for food, cereal crops such as emmer, bread wheat and barley were grown. Hunting, too, was an important source of food, but cattle and horses were also used for meat. By the end of the period, some 4,000 years ago, horses and oxen were being used as draught animals rather than for food.

Farming tools also improved. The use of the plough became widespread, which made it possible to cultivate more ground. This, in turn, meant a better food supply and the population increased.

Axes for felling trees and spades for digging the ground also improved. The increasing use of metal helped in this, particularly when a sharp edge was needed, as in the sickles used for harvesting.

The Unetice culture

The Unetice culture gets its name from the site in Czechoslovakia where it was first studied, but it was common throughout Europe during the Bronze Age. These people were good potters, for many fine clay bowls and urns have been found. Many of the villages were situated near farm land and usually consisted of a few timber houses.

Lake-dwellers of Bronze Age Europe

Lakeside communities were common in eastern France, Switzerland and northern Italy. They were often quite large by the standards of the time, with as many as 50 people living in them. The rectangular houses were made of wood and thatched with reeds gathered from the lake. Sometimes the settlements developed in a haphazard fashion, but in others there are definite signs that the houses were built in neat rows.

Developing technology and trade

As the period progressed, metal tools and vessels gradually replaced those made of wood or stone.

This rapidly improving technology, together with improvements in agriculture, led to an increase in population. This, in turn, brought greater social stratification and with it came conflict between different groups. The increasing use of metal had the unfortunate side effect of producing much better, and therefore much more dangerous, weapons.

The wheel also appeared at this time, and meant that land communications became easier, opening up the way for trade. Sea trade also developed, and there was an extensive network of trade routes from the Black Sea in the east to the Atlantic in the west, and to the Mediterranean in the south.

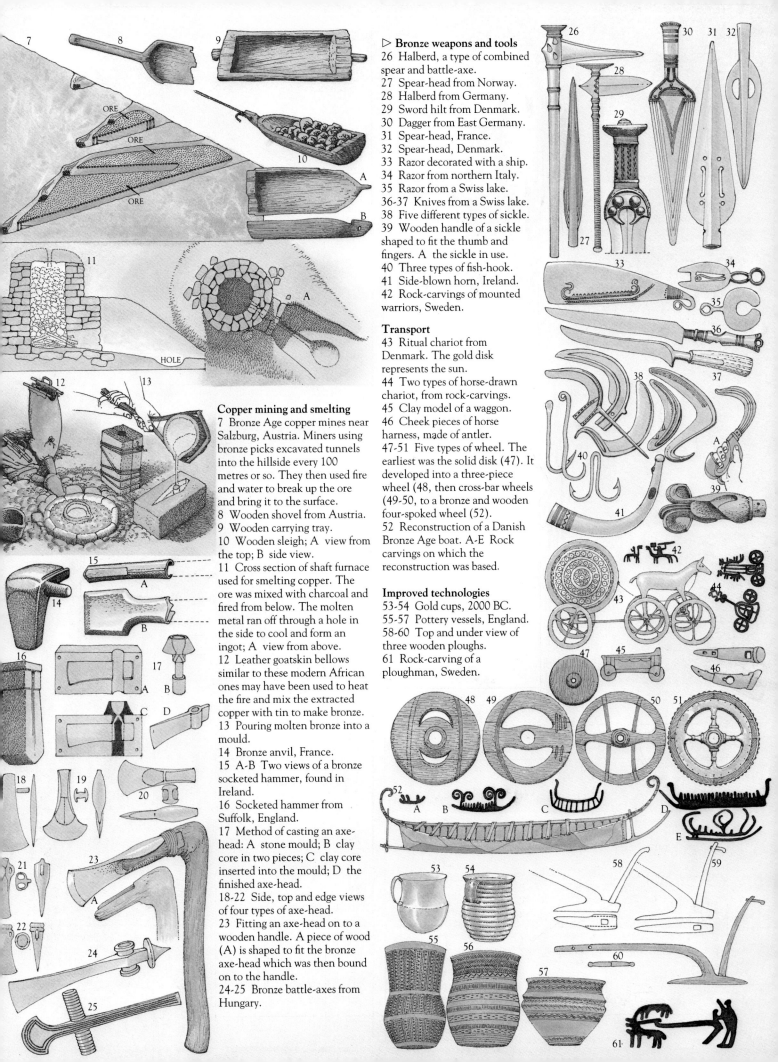

Bronze weapons and tools
26 Halberd, a type of combined spear and battle-axe.
27 Spear-head from Norway.
28 Halberd from Germany.
29 Sword hilt from Denmark.
30 Dagger from East Germany.
31 Spear-head, France.
32 Spear-head, Denmark.
33 Razor decorated with a ship.
34 Razor from northern Italy.
35 Razor from a Swiss lake.
36-37 Knives from a Swiss lake.
38 Five different types of sickle.
39 Wooden handle of a sickle shaped to fit the thumb and fingers. A the sickle in use.
40 Three types of fish-hook.
41 Side-blown horn, Ireland.
42 Rock-carvings of mounted warriors, Sweden.

Transport
43 Ritual chariot from Denmark. The gold disk represents the sun.
44 Two types of horse-drawn chariot, from rock-carvings.
45 Clay model of a waggon.
46 Cheek pieces of horse harness, made of antler.
47-51 Five types of wheel. The earliest was the solid disk (47). It developed into a three-piece wheel (48, then cross-bar wheels (49-50, to a bronze and wooden four-spoked wheel (52).
52 Reconstruction of a Danish Bronze Age boat. A-E Rock carvings on which the reconstruction was based.

Improved technologies
53-54 Gold cups, 2000 BC.
55-57 Pottery vessels, England.
58-60 Top and under view of three wooden ploughs.
61 Rock-carving of a ploughman, Sweden.

Copper mining and smelting
7 Bronze Age copper mines near Salzburg, Austria. Miners using bronze picks excavated tunnels into the hillside every 100 metres or so. They then used fire and water to break up the ore and bring it to the surface.
8 Wooden shovel from Austria.
9 Wooden carrying tray.
10 Wooden sleigh; A view from the top; B side view.
11 Cross section of shaft furnace used for smelting copper. The ore was mixed with charcoal and fired from below. The molten metal ran off through a hole in the side to cool and form an ingot; A view from above.
12 Leather goatskin bellows similar to these modern African ones may have been used to heat the fire and mix the extracted copper with tin to make bronze.
13 Pouring molten bronze into a mould.
14 Bronze anvil, France.
15 A-B Two views of a bronze socketed hammer, found in Ireland.
16 Socketed hammer from Suffolk, England.
17 Method of casting an axe-head: A stone mould; B clay core in two pieces; C clay core inserted into the mould; D the finished axe-head.
18-22 Side, top and edge views of four types of axe-head.
23 Fitting an axe-head on to a wooden handle. A piece of wood (A) is shaped to fit the bronze axe-head which was then bound on to the handle.
24-25 Bronze battle-axes from Hungary.

A Chinese pavilion

Chinese civilization has a longer continuous history than any other in the world today. Although civilization as we know it first began in the Middle East, the civilizations of that area have long since disappeared, while China's still survives.

The Shang civilization

Quite suddenly, and it would appear quite independently of other developments, about 4,000 years ago, a civilization that historians call the 'Shang' arose north of the Yellow River, in the present district of Anyang. Chinese tradition mentions an earlier dynasty, the Hsia, but archaeologists have found no trace of it. Probably it was a Neolithic culture which laid the foundations for the craft skills which blossomed in the Shang period.

Little is known about Shang society. Although the remains of buildings give some clues, the best sources of information are the cemeteries. In the cemetery at Anyang there were over a thousand graves, as well as the 'Royal Tombs'.

A royal burial

The earliest royal tombs, which were the largest, were dug in the shape of a cross. Four staircases or ramps descended into the chamber where the coffin was put on a platform of richly carved stone. In one tomb nine guards and nine dogs had been killed and placed around the platform on which the coffin of the dead prince rested. Bronze and jade objects, musical instruments and pottery jars were placed in rows at the bottom of the staircases, together with ten human heads. Nearby was a chariot, its four horses slaughtered together with three armed warriors.

Weapons and war

War was common in early China, just as it was to be in later times. The bronze halberd was the Shang warrior's most important weapon, together with the bow and arrow. The bow was short and powerful, especially useful for mounted soldiers, and fired arrows with heavy bronze heads. Bows of the kind used in the Shang period seem to have originated in Neolithic Siberia.

The end of the beginning

The Shang rulers held power over the peoples of the Yellow River valley until 1027 BC. Then, the ruler of the neighbouring state of Ch'in defeated the armies of the Shang ruler in battle. Under the Ch'in emperor Shin-Huang-Ti, China became a powerful empire and the Great Wall was built, but it was the Shang who had first started China on the road of civilization.

A royal tomb
1 The royal tomb of the late Shang period, c. 1100 BC, found near Anyang.
2 Plan of the tomb.
3 'Music Stone' found in the tomb which made a noise when struck.
4 Shang chariot yoke.
5 Dragon-shaped chariot decorations.
6 Part of a bronze yoke.
7 Position of the chariot, charioteer and two horses found in the tomb.
8 Harness cheek-piece, c. 800 BC.
9 Chariot axle-cap and linch-pin.
10 Bronze bridle-piece, c. 700 BC.

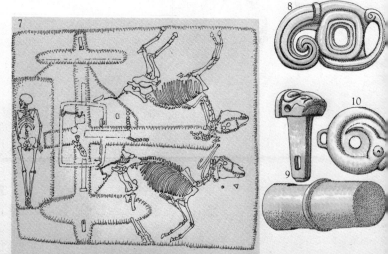

▽ A royal palace

A reconstruction of the royal Shang palace or 'pavilion' which was excavated at Pan-Lung-Cheng. It measured 39.8 metres in length and 12.3 metres wide. Built on an earth terrace to raise it above the level of other buildings, it had four chambers in the centre of a maze of surrounding and interconnecting corridors. The roof had multiple eaves, as shown in the illustration, and was probably thatched.

What the palace was used for is a puzzle. It does not really seem to have been a place to live in. Some archaeologists believe that it was a sort of temple and that religious worship and rituals went on in the four central chambers. The beautiful bronze vessels found at the site are used as evidence in support of this theory.

It is also difficult to know what the pavilion looked like inside. Because it was an important building it probably had decorated walls but how they were decorated – whether by painting or with tapestries – remains a mystery. It is sad, too, for our knowledge of the Shang period, that if the palace ever contained furniture this also has vanished.

▷ Bronze Age China

The extent of the Chinese empire about 4,000 years ago. The earliest known civilization in China started on the fertile northern plains around the Huang-Ho river. The earliest capital of the Shang rulers was at Cheng-Chou, but later emperors moved the centre of the government to the more northerly city of Anyang.

From the small area shown on the map, China grew over the centuries into the vast country it is today.

Shang warriors and their weapons

11 Shang pictograms, as well as other remains, give many clues about the weapons and armour used by Shang soldiers. The dagger-axe, an early form of halberd, was the principal weapon. The soldiers were protected by a helmet and plated armour, and carried a shield as well as their weapons.

12 Pictogram of soldier with halberd and shield.

13 Pictogram showing axe used for beheading ritual victims.

14 Pictogram of a halberd.

15 Pictogram of a soldier with a halberd.

16 Bronze Shang helmet found at Anyang. The socket on the top was to hold a decorative plume.

17 Reconstruction of a Shang war-chariot and prince charioteer.

18 Pictogram showing a building with a roof similar to that of the Shang royal palace (above).

19 Curved knife made of bronze; A pictogram of a similar weapon.

20 Bronze halberd.

21 Halberd of jade in a beautifully decorated bronze holder. Halberds as fine as this are believed to have been used for ceremonies and rituals.

22 Plain jade halberd.

23-25 Three different types of arrowhead, all made in bronze.

26 Pictogram of a bow and arrow of the type used by the Shang armies. There is evidence of similar bows from Siberia.

27-28 Two different designs of spearhead. They are socketed so that they fit securely over the end of a wooden spear-shaft.

29 Ceremonial axe-head of bronze. The fine quality of the decoration suggests that it was used for ceremonies and important occasions; it was probably never meant to be used in battle.

30 Two views of a plain, socketed axe-head.

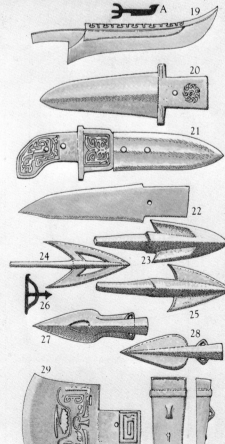

The first Chinese writing

Writing is always one of the first signs of a settled and developed society.

In China writing started during the Shang period. It took the form of ideograms, from which modern Chinese writing derives. The first inscriptions were done on the shoulder blades of pigs and oxen or on the shells of tortoises. Large numbers of these have been discovered at Anyang, preserved in what archaeologists believe may have been libraries. The inscriptions are difficult to understand, but were probably concerned with rituals of some kind.

Scientists have identified about 5,000 different ideograms, about half of which are directly related to modern Chinese writing.

The layout of a Shang city

A Shang city has been excavated at Cheng-Chou. The centre of the city was roughly rectangular – 2 kilometres from north to south and 1.7 kilometres from east to west. The city was surrounded by an earth wall which was 20 metres wide at the base. The houses were laid out in parallel streets. Some of the important buildings, like temples or palaces, were raised on platforms (see page 37). As happend later in Peking, the city walls had lookout towers for defence.

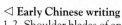
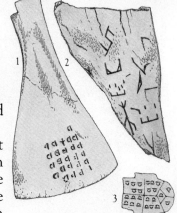

◁ **Early Chinese writing**
1-2 Shoulder blades of animals were inscribed with magic symbols and used to foretell the future.
3 Tortoiseshells were also used to foretell the future.
4 These pictograms are the direct ancestors of modern Chinese scripts.

▷ **Ornaments**
5 Comb made of bone.
6 The head of a very finely carved bone hairpin.
7 Head of a carved bone hairpin. The quality of the carving shows that the Shang craftsmen were not just skilled in metalwork; A the whole pin.
8 Two views of a plainer bone hairpin.
9 Carved jade amulet.
10 Jade hairpin showing the profile of a woman and suggesting a very elaborate headdress or hairstyle; A a possible reconstruction of that hairstyle.

◁ **A Chinese ritual**
The Shang people practised many elaborate rituals. The scene on the left is a reconstruction of what one such ceremony may have looked like. Beautiful bronze vessels to hold food and wine were used to appease the spirits of the dead. The costumes are based on small carved jade figures dating from Shang times.

▽ **Bronze ritual vessels**
These are just a few of the many fine bronze vessels found by archaeologists dating from Shang times. The names are those by which they are called in Chinese.
11 Lei vessel; 12 P'an; 13 Ting; 14-15 Chüeh; 16 Tsün; 17 Yü; 18 Li; 19 Kuei; 20 Hsien; 21 Ting; 22 bronze bell.

The potter's work
23 Clay vase with carved decoration.
24-25 Glazed earthenware jars.
26 Pottery kiln.
27 Earthenware Chüeh jug.
28 Earthenware jar.
29 Vase with rounded base.
30 Another type of pottery kiln.

Agricultural implements
31 Hand quern for grinding corn. Although this is modern, similar querns were used in Shang times.
32 Rotary flail for threshing grain. It is made of bamboo.
33 Hoe; A the hoe blade without a handle.
34 Simple plough pulled by a man.
35 Sickles of different types.
36 Grubbing fork.
All these tools are modern, but similar to earlier ones.

Bronze casting
37 Cross-section through a mould used for casting bronze. The vessel being made is upside-down and the molten bronze runs into the mould via the legs of the vessel; A cross section of the mould showing the legs of the vessel; B cross section through the mould showing the shape of the vessel in dark brown.

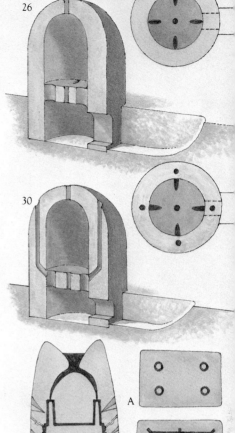

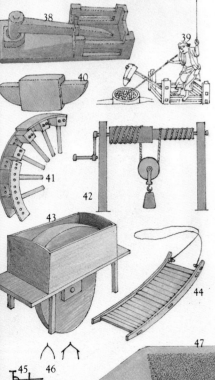

Shang technology
38 Clay model of a man-powered tilt hammer.
39 Picture of this type of tilt-hammer in action.
40 Modern anvil, another simple piece of technology the Shangs may have known.
41 Diagram of how a Chinese cartwheel was made.
42 The differential, or Chinese, windlass for lifting heavy objects.
43 Reconstruction of a Chinese wheelbarrow.
44 Sledge used to carry mud for building work.
45 Shang pictogram of a carpenter.
46 Pictograms of two different kinds of building.
47 Section of a Shang city based on excavations at Anyang.
48 Reconstruction of a house.

Craftsmanship in bronze
The people of Cheng-Chou were skilled craftsmen. Bronze was discovered at the very beginning of the Shang period and a thriving tradition of bronze-working developed – a tradition which has continued throughout Chinese civilization. Some of the items found here are exceptionally fine.

Outside the city wall at Cheng-Chou were two areas where the bronze workers lived and worked. Archaeologists can tell this from the remains they have excavated: foundries, slag from the furnaces, oxidized copper (copper is used in the making of bronze), pouring beakers, moulds and some of the objects which were being made in the workshops.

These included very elaborate vessels, obviously intended for princes and other royalty. There were also beakers and jugs that may have been for use in the temples, as well as smaller, more ordinary items such as bowls and jars.

An archaeological mystery
It is difficult to explain this sudden rise of a highly developed, highly skilled metalworking industry, especially as it was apparently not influenced either by an earlier civilization or a neighbouring society. It remains a mystery to archaeologists.

The Etruscans

The Etruscans were the first civilized people of western Europe. From the eighth to the third centuries BC they lived in central Italy, in a region known as Etruria, between the modern cities of Florence and Rome, and enclosed by the rivers Arno and Tiber and the Tyrrhenian Sea.

Almost all Etruscan towns grew up on the sites of much older settlements. In fact, by the 10th century BC, many prehistoric settlements in Etruria were large enough to be called towns. Some of these settlements gradually developed into cities. The coastal towns were the first to expand as traders, mainly from the eastern Mediterranean, the Aegean and Phoenicia, came to do business in the towns. When, in the 10th or 9th century BC, iron was discovered in the hills of southern Etruria, trade increased enormously. In later times Phoenicians and Greeks even had their own quarters and temples in Etruscan coastal towns.

The iron trade soon brought wealth to the ruling Etruscan families. As a result, they started to extend their power over inland farming regions as far north as the Po valley.

The communities along the coast spread inland, too, and settlements there in turn developed into cities.

The political structure of Etruria

Etruscan civilization was based on a small number of aristocratic families, who ruled over quite independent city-states. There was no political unity, and it was only their sense of sharing a culture and religion that held these city-states together.

As a result, when the city-states were later attacked by the strong and well-organised state of Rome, they could not defend themselves and were soon overwhelmed by their thrusting neighbour. Under the dominance of Rome, Etruscan civilization disappeared almost without trace.

An Etruscan palace

The reconstruction opposite shows the palace of an Etruscan nobleman. It was built in central Etruria during the 7th century BC and destroyed a little more than a century later by unknown raiders.

The noblemen ruled their city-states from palaces like this. From here they administered the law, settled disputes and probably collected taxes. They had control over every aspect of their subjects' lives, a control which may well have extended to the power of life and death. Those Romans who were wealthy enough to own slaves certainly regarded this power as their right where slaves were concerned, so it is quite likely that the earlier Etruscans, who also used slave labour, followed the same practice.

An Etruscan nobleman at home
1 Terracotta wall-tile from an Etruscan palace/sanctuary near Siena dating from the middle of the 6th century BC. It shows a lady with her maid.
2 Reconstructed scene of a nobleman, his wife and a maidservant. It is based on the tile (1). The chairs were made of wickerwork. Archaeologists do not know what the bucket the maid carries was used for.
3 Boot worn by an Etruscan man in the 6th century BC.
4 Lady's slipper of the same period.
5 Hairpin found at a site near Siena.
6-7 Gold earrings, showing the skill of the Etruscan goldsmiths.
8 Two views of a pin used to fasten clothes.
9 Small pottery container used to hold oil and perfumes.
10 Small alabaster jar also used for holding perfumes and oils.
11 Noblewoman's headdress and hairstyle, based on a statue from the Etruscan site of Chiusi.
12 Terracotta wall-tile showing a procession. There is a reconstruction of this scene at the bottom of the opposite page.

▷ **Terracotta roofing**
19 Decorative terracotta end-tile. These tiles were used along the eaves of important buildings. This one is decorated with the head of a gorgon – a mythical creature.
20 Detail of the roof construction, showing the curved and flat tiles and the decorative end-tile in position.
21 End-tile decorated with the head of a rabbit.
22 Man's head used as a decoration on an end-tile. These two tiles (21-22) are less elaborate than 18, where the decorative moulding was painted.

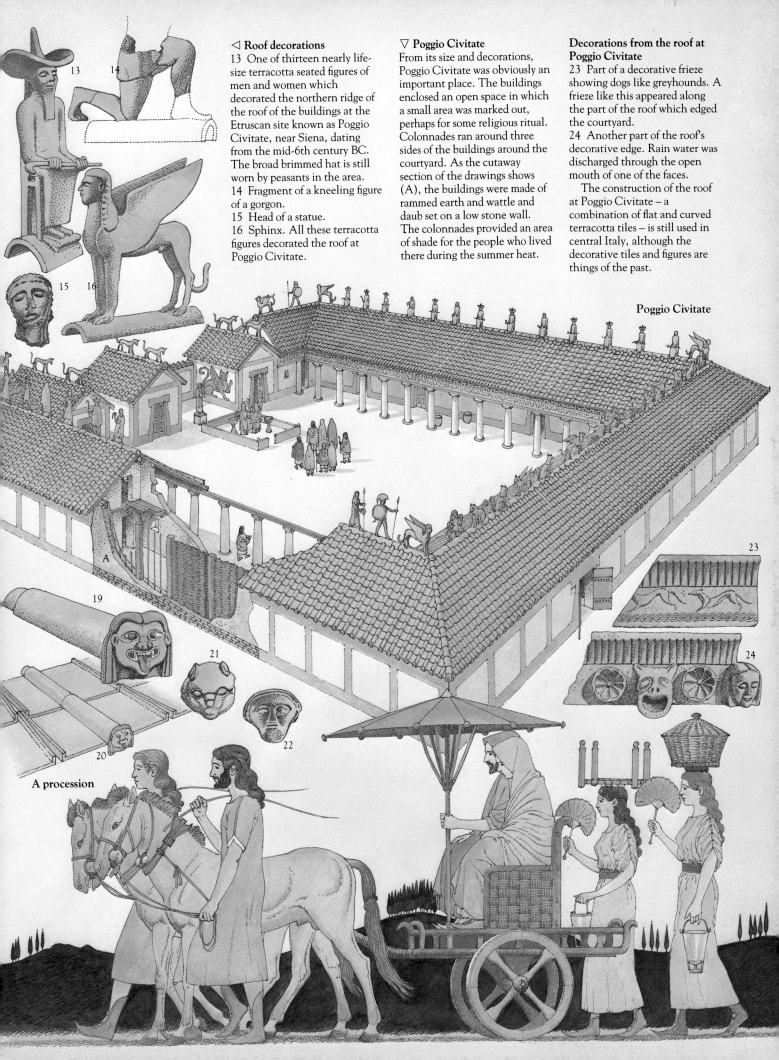

◁ **Roof decorations**
13 One of thirteen nearly life-size terracotta seated figures of men and women which decorated the northern ridge of the roof of the buildings at the Etruscan site known as Poggio Civitate, near Siena, dating from the mid-6th century BC. The broad brimmed hat is still worn by peasants in the area.
14 Fragment of a kneeling figure of a gorgon.
15 Head of a statue.
16 Sphinx. All these terracotta figures decorated the roof at Poggio Civitate.

▽ **Poggio Civitate**
From its size and decorations, Poggio Civitate was obviously an important place. The buildings enclosed an open space in which a small area was marked out, perhaps for some religious ritual. Colonnades ran around three sides of the buildings around the courtyard. As the cutaway section of the drawings shows (A), the buildings were made of rammed earth and wattle and daub set on a low stone wall. The colonnades provided an area of shade for the people who lived there during the summer heat.

Decorations from the roof at Poggio Civitate
23 Part of a decorative frieze showing dogs like greyhounds. A frieze like this appeared along the part of the roof which edged the courtyard.
24 Another part of the roof's decorative edge. Rain water was discharged through the open mouth of one of the faces.

The construction of the roof at Poggio Civitate – a combination of flat and curved terracotta tiles – is still used in central Italy, although the decorative tiles and figures are things of the past.

Poggio Civitate

A procession

Clues to Etruscan life

Etruscan tombs from southern Etruria provide more evidence about their homes than the few houses that survive.

1 The 'Tomba dei Capitelli' at Caere (modern Cerveteri) gives a good idea of the interior of a sixth-century BC Etruscan home.

2 A ground plan of the tomb.

3 Small terracotta urn to hold the ashes of a dead person.

4 Etruscan funeral urn, seventh-century BC. It represents a one-roomed house with the thatch held down with wooden poles.

5 Reconstruction of a house excavated near Viterbo; A plan of the house.

6-7 Ground plans of other houses at the same site.

8 Painted tile from Acquarossa; it was used to decorate the lower edge of the roof.

9 Decorative ridge tile also from Acquarossa.

10 Clay water-supply pipes from Marzabotto, near Bologna.

11 Two views of a mound tomb typical of northern Etruria.

12 Clay coffin representing a funeral bed with the dead person on it.

13 Carved stone ash urn.

14 A tombstone from northern Etruria.

15 Reconstruction of the temple at Veii, dating from the sixth century BC; A ground plan of the temple.

16 Bronze candle-holder.

17 Bronze tripod used in temples.

18 Bronze model of a sheep's liver used by priests in religious ceremonies.

19 Boundary stone used to mark the edge of a sacred area.

20-21 Bronze rattle showing a weaver at work.

22 Clay reel for thread.

23 Spindle whorl used in spinning thread.

24-26 Three different types of pottery vessel.

27 Stand used to store clay vessels in the home.

A mysterious language

Archaeologists have managed to piece together quite a lot of information about the Etruscans and their way of life, but very little is known about their language. They had a literature, but only a few inscriptions on tombs and vases have survived, which has made deciphering the language very difficult.

As a result, we know very little about what the Etruscans thought, or what their literature, poetry or theatre was like. They certainly had these arts, for it would have been quite exceptional for a civilization as advanced as theirs in other ways not to have had a thriving cultural tradition as well.

Houses and tombs

Most of what we do know about the Etruscans comes, in fact, from excavations of their tombs.

Etruscan tombs usually repeat the design of Etruscan houses. Some of the tombs were dug into volcanic rock (tufa), others were built above ground and covered with earth to form an artificial mound, or even a small hill.

These tombs were all furnished with the most valuable belongings of the dead person. These included beautiful metal vessels, delicate models of fine furniture, and, of course, a great deal of precious jewellery. All these objects have helped archaeologists to build up a picture of Etruscan domestic life.

Pottery skills

It was, however, in pottery that the Etruscans really excelled. They fashioned lifesize statues or coffins which are extremely fine and realistic portraits of the people for whom they were made. The beautiful pottery bowls, jars and other vessels which have been found in the tombs also testify to the considerable skill of the Etruscan craftsmen potters.

Etruscan art has a special power and beauty of its own, which owes little to any influence from the Greeks or other peoples of the eastern Mediterranean.

The beginnings of Rome

Rome, which was to become the most powerful state in the ancient world, started as an Etruscan city. Sited on the southern border of Etruria, it grew up at a crossing-point on the River Tiber. In such a position it became a rich business centre for Greeks, Sicilians and traders from the south of Italy. As a result it became increasingly powerful and soon outgrew its ties with the Etruscan state.

In one of the many periods of inter-city squabbles, Rome's rulers severed their links with Etruria. A few centuries later, in the third century BC, Rome absorbed the Etruscan city-states into its own growing territory. In turn, Etruscan culture survived and lived on in the civilization of the Roman Empire.

▷ **The Etruscan nation**
This map shows the extent of the Etruscan nation (in red) and its cultural and political expansion in the sixth century BC (in orange). Although their artefacts reached all over Italy and the rest of Europe, the political influence of the Etruscans was never very great beyond the south of Rome. Surprisingly, although probably due to trading links, there was an area around Naples which seems to have been influenced by the Etruscans. The map shows the most important Etruscan cities.

▽ **The Etruscan alphabet** (28) as it was in the sixth century BC. It is a modified form of Greek, the differences reflecting different pronounciations.

28

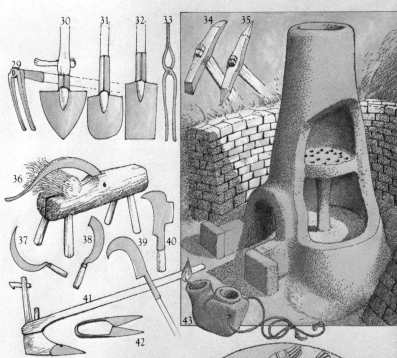

Etruscan metalwork
29 Two-pronged hoe.
30 Spade with a foot-rest.
31-32 Spades.
33 Blacksmith's tongs.
34-35 Miners' picks.
36 Fodder cutter. Similar tools are still used in Tuscany today.
37-38 Two different types of sickle.
39-40 Bill-hooks.
41 Etruscan plough.
42 Shears which could be used with one hand.
43 Reconstruction of a furnace for smelting iron, excavated near Populonia.
44 Bronze panel from the side of a chariot.

The Greeks at home

The influence of the beliefs, ideas and attitudes of the Ancient Greeks is still felt today. The Greeks believed they were different from any other people they knew, and divided the world into two groups: the 'Hellenes' (as they called themselves) and the 'barbarians' which covered everybody who was not a Greek. The reason for this was that the Greeks felt that they were free while everyone else was living in slavery. Unlike anywhere else at the time, Greek society was ruled by law which upheld justice and was known to all the people. A Greek felt that he was a member of the state and not a subject whose fate was in the hands of a despot. The concept of democracy, with all citizens having a say in how the state was run, originated in Ancient Greece.

The rise of the city-states

The emerging Greek civilization was based on a series of city-states. This was largely dictated by the geography of the country: Greece is very mountainous with a complex coastline on both the mainland and the islands. Inland, small fertile plains are separated from one another by mountain ridges which keep them quite isolated, particularly during the winter when land communications are difficult. In these plains cities developed as autonomous political and religious units.

Athens

Athens was the most important city mainly because its territory was larger, although still small by modern standards. Its population was probably about a quarter of a million. Around the city and as far as the mountains were scattered villages, hamlets and farms.

Greek society

The city-states had distinct social classes, but in all classes the basic social unit was the family.

The wives of middle and upper-class men led secluded lives. There was even a special room in the house set aside for them. This was the 'gynaeceum', which was on the first floor of the house close to the 'thalamos', the room for the husband and wife. Women of the lower classes enjoyed more freedom, as their homes were too small to have a gynaeceum.

Greek homes

Houses were quite small, and were built of wood, brick or a mixture of pebbles and baked earth. There was no glass in the small windows, which were closed with wooden shutters in the winter. Kitchens were rare, and most food was cooked outside in the open air.

Women's clothes and jewellery
1 Women sewing. They are sitting on folding stools around a small table. The Ionian chitons they are wearing were introduced in the sixth century BC.
2 The Ionian chiton was a rectangular piece of cloth about 1.50 metres wide and 3 metres long. The material was folded as shown, fastened with pins ('fibulae') along the arms and then belted around the waist.
3 The Dorian chiton was more elaborate, but was held by only two pins at the shoulders.
4 Woman wearing a Dorian chiton with the waist girdle over the fold.
5 Gold snake bracelet.
6 A simpler way of wearing the Dorian chiton.
7 Pin used to fasten hair bands.
8 Golden earring, c. 450 BC.
9 Gold fibula, c. 500 BC.
10 Gold necklace from Athens.
11 Gold earring, c. 350 BC.
12 Two women wearing the peplos, a square woollen mantle, over their chitons. The seated woman is rolling wool across her leg before spinning it.

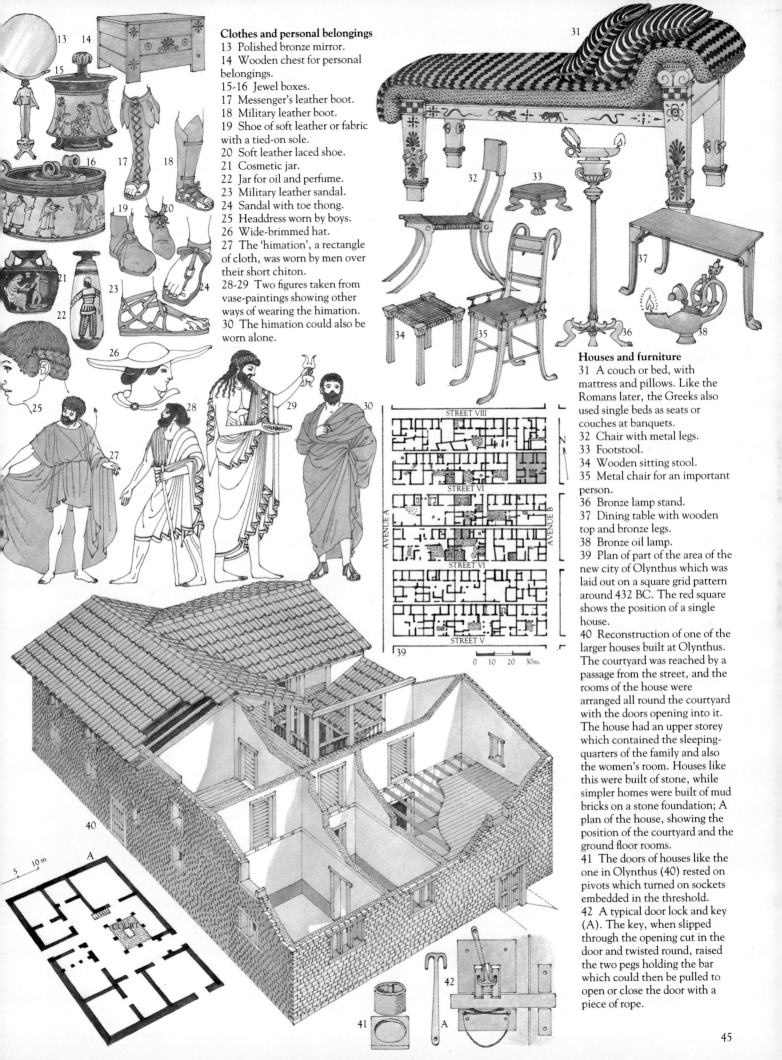

Clothes and personal belongings

13 Polished bronze mirror.
14 Wooden chest for personal belongings.
15-16 Jewel boxes.
17 Messenger's leather boot.
18 Military leather boot.
19 Shoe of soft leather or fabric with a tied-on sole.
20 Soft leather laced shoe.
21 Cosmetic jar.
22 Jar for oil and perfume.
23 Military leather sandal.
24 Sandal with toe thong.
25 Headdress worn by boys.
26 Wide-brimmed hat.
27 The 'himation', a rectangle of cloth, was worn by men over their short chiton.
28-29 Two figures taken from vase-paintings showing other ways of wearing the himation.
30 The himation could also be worn alone.

Houses and furniture

31 A couch or bed, with mattress and pillows. Like the Romans later, the Greeks also used single beds as seats or couches at banquets.
32 Chair with metal legs.
33 Footstool.
34 Wooden sitting stool.
35 Metal chair for an important person.
36 Bronze lamp stand.
37 Dining table with wooden top and bronze legs.
38 Bronze oil lamp.
39 Plan of part of the area of the new city of Olynthus which was laid out on a square grid pattern around 432 BC. The red square shows the position of a single house.
40 Reconstruction of one of the larger houses built at Olynthus. The courtyard was reached by a passage from the street, and the rooms of the house were arranged all round the courtyard with the doors opening into it. The house had an upper storey which contained the sleeping-quarters of the family and also the women's room. Houses like this were built of stone, while simpler homes were built of mud bricks on a stone foundation; A plan of the house, showing the position of the courtyard and the ground floor rooms.
41 The doors of houses like the one in Olynthus (40) rested on pivots which turned on sockets embedded in the threshold.
42 A typical door lock and key (A). The key, when slipped through the opening cut in the door and twisted round, raised the two pegs holding the bar which could then be pulled to open or close the door with a piece of rope.

STREET VIII

STREET VI

AVENUE A

AVENUE B

STREET VI

STREET V

0 10 20 30m.

39

COURT

5   10 m

A

42

41

A

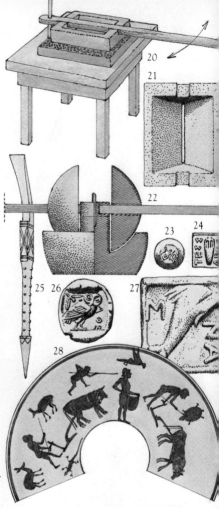

◁ **Spinning and weaving**
1 Woman spinning wool.
2 Typical Greek loom drawn from a vase painting.
3 Before the wool was spun the fibres were separated by rubbing them over the 'epinetron'. This semi-cylindrical clay implement was placed over the knee.
4 Clay spindle-whorl (or weight).
5 Top of an ivory spindle whorl.
6 Iron scissors.
7 Bronze thimble.
8 Bronze needle with two eyes.
9 Bronze spindle.
10-11 Two kinds of loom weight.
12 Bronze loom shuttle.

◁ **Toys and games**
13 The Ancient Greek alphabet, with modern sounds shown in the Latin alphabet below.
14 A-B Two views of knucklebones. The object of the game was to throw them in the air and catch them on the back of the hand.
15 A-B Ivory dice.
16 Decorated clay top.
17 Clay doll.
18 Woman with child in a high-chair.
19 Boys playing with toy chariots, from a jug (A).

THE GREEKS AT HOME

Greek towns

During the fourth century BC the Greeks began to plan their towns and settlements on a rational basis. This was, of course, only possible when they were building a completely new settlement; wherever there had been an older community the new buildings just grew up around it. In the new towns, however, they were able to take into consideration such things as exposure to sunlight, wind direction, conditions for access and good drainage.

A well-planned town

Priene, on the coast of Asia Minor (modern Turkey), is an excellent example of a planned Greek town. Historically it is of little importance, but it is one of the best examples of how a rational method of square grid planning was applied successfully to a very difficult site.

The town is perched on a steep hill, many of the cross streets were steep flights of steps, but the principal streets were designed to run along the slope and were wider than the others. The market place ('agora') occupied a central terraced area and was overlooked by the theatre and the magnificent temple of Athene – one of the Greeks' principal goddesses. The 'acropolis' (fortified citadel) towered 300 metres above the town, offering a splendid vantage point.

Farming in Ancient Greece

Agriculture in Greece was, and still is, very laborious. The rains in the autumn and winter and the droughts in summer mean that the soil must constantly be broken up, either to absorb the moisture, or else to retain it and stop the soil from drying out completely. In early times a crop was usually obtained from a field every other year. The next year the field would be ploughed up and allowed to rest until the next growing season.

Ploughing and sowing were usually done in the autumn. Wheat was the chief cereal crop, although barley was important in the Athens area. These crops were harvested in May. Then, in September, it was time to harvest the grapes – another important crop.

Oxen were used to pull the ploughs, and heavy goods were transported by pack mules over the difficult, mountainous countryside.

Food

Goats were kept to provide both milk and cheese. Meat was a rare luxury, only eaten on special occasions and after religious rituals. Fish, however, was a common dish. Bread was as important then as it is today, and wine was the chief drink. However, as still in southern European countries, the Greeks did not drink wine neat; instead they mixed it with water.

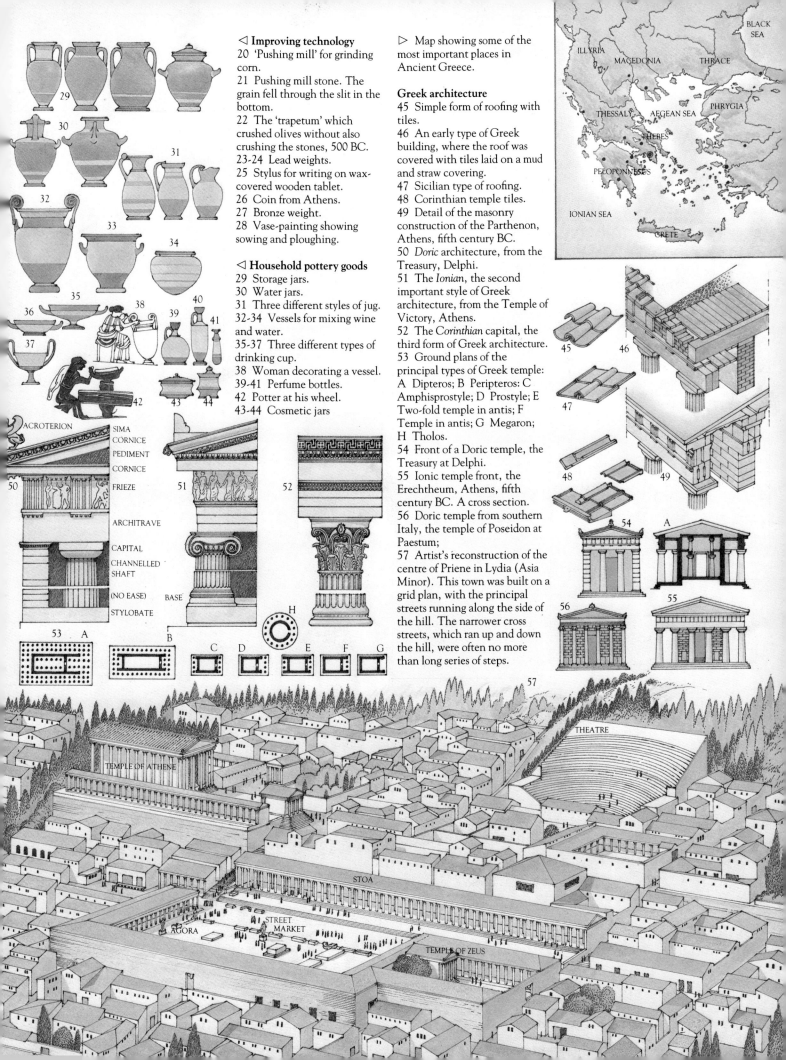

BLACK SEA

ILLYRIA
MACEDONIA   THRACE
THESSALY   AEGEAN SEA   PHRYGIA
THEBES
PELOPONNESES
IONIAN SEA
CRETE

◁ **Improving technology**
20 'Pushing mill' for grinding corn.
21 Pushing mill stone. The grain fell through the slit in the bottom.
22 The 'trapetum' which crushed olives without also crushing the stones, 500 BC.
23-24 Lead weights.
25 Stylus for writing on wax-covered wooden tablet.
26 Coin from Athens.
27 Bronze weight.
28 Vase-painting showing sowing and ploughing.

◁ **Household pottery goods**
29 Storage jars.
30 Water jars.
31 Three different styles of jug.
32-34 Vessels for mixing wine and water.
35-37 Three different types of drinking cup.
38 Woman decorating a vessel.
39-41 Perfume bottles.
42 Potter at his wheel.
43-44 Cosmetic jars

▷ Map showing some of the most important places in Ancient Greece.

Greek architecture
45 Simple form of roofing with tiles.
46 An early type of Greek building, where the roof was covered with tiles laid on a mud and straw covering.
47 Sicilian type of roofing.
48 Corinthian temple tiles.
49 Detail of the masonry construction of the Parthenon, Athens, fifth century BC.
50 *Doric* architecture, from the Treasury, Delphi.
51 The *Ionian*, the second important style of Greek architecture, from the Temple of Victory, Athens.
52 The *Corinthian* capital, the third form of Greek architecture.
53 Ground plans of the principal types of Greek temple: A Dipteros; B Peripteros: C Amphisprostyle; D Prostyle; E Two-fold temple in antis; F Temple in antis; G Megaron; H Tholos.
54 Front of a Doric temple, the Treasury at Delphi.
55 Ionic temple front, the Erechtheum, Athens, fifth century BC. A cross section.
56 Doric temple from southern Italy, the temple of Poseidon at Paestum;
57 Artist's reconstruction of the centre of Priene in Lydia (Asia Minor). This town was built on a grid plan, with the principal streets running along the side of the hill. The narrower cross streets, which ran up and down the hill, were often no more than long series of steps.

ACROTERION
SIMA
CORNICE
PEDIMENT
CORNICE
FRIEZE
ARCHITRAVE
CAPITAL
CHANNELLED SHAFT
(NO EASE)
BASE
STYLOBATE

TEMPLE OF ATHENE
THEATRE
STOA
STREET MARKET
AGORA
TEMPLE OF ZEUS

A brief chronology

4,000,000 years ago: some primates in Africa started walking on two legs.

4,000,000–35,000 B.C. THE EARLIEST TOOLMAKERS (page 4)

In this period there were four great Ice Ages followed by temperate periods during which man evolved, developing increasingly sophisticated tools of stone and spreading from Africa across Europe and Asia, and thence to the Americas and Australia.

35,000–10,000 B.C. THE ICE-AGE HUNTERS (page 8)

Around 10,000 B.C. the ice withdrew and gradually the Earth's climate became like today's. This caused dramatic changes in culture and technology. The Old Stone Age gave way to the Middle Stone Age, or Mesolithic culture, which lasted in Northern Europe until around 2,000 B.C.

10,000 to 5,000 B.C. THE FISHER HUNTERS (page 12)

In warmer areas, such as the Middle East, Mesolithic culture gave way very quickly to urban life and a totally different economic system.

7,000 B.C. ÇATAL HÜYÜK: THE FIRST CITY (page 16)

The Neolithic Period, or New Stone Age, brought widespread technological and social change: the discovery of pottery, weaving and the cultivation and domestication of wild plants and animals.

6,000 B.C. THE FIRST FOOD PRODUCERS (page 20)

The division of labour which had gradually taken place since the Mesolithic Period led to the development of advanced civilizations. Changes in the economy freed part of the population from working in the fields, and more people became available to perform functions such as religion, defence, administration and building.

2,500 B.C. THE CRAFTSMEN OF EGYPT (page 24)

An important aspect of civilization is the growth of the city. Trade was probably the chief element which brought civilization from Turkey and Egypt to the island of Crete and to the Greek mainland around 2,600 B.C.

1,570 B.C. MINOAN CRETE (page 28)

Around 1,500 B.C. the late Neolithic peoples of Western Europe acquired the use of bronze, which had been known in the Mediterranean and Eastern Europe since 3,500 B.C., and established trade across the continent.

1,200 B.C. PEOPLE OF THE NORTH (page 32)

At the same time Chinese farmers in Honan established a feudal state and started building large cities on a square grid plan. The Chinese, independently, developed bronze-working and writing.

1,200 B.C. A CHINESE PAVILION (page 36)

The Aryans, a people of Indo-European origin, migrated into the Ganges valley, dominating the original inhabitants. The Greeks migrated to Greece from the north, driving the Achaeans away. These warriors were mounted on horses and carried weapons of iron. The Iron Age saw the development of the Etruscan culture in Central Italy, from 900 B.C.

600 B.C. THE ETRUSCANS (page 40)

In 750 B.C. the Greeks started to establish colonies in southern Italy; urban development and writing spread across Italy, and Rome was founded on the banks of the Tiber. Between 406 and 396 B.C. the Romans defeated the Etruscans and started the conquest of northern Italy.

400 to 300 B.C. THE GREEKS AT HOME (page 44)

There was intermittent fighting between the Greek city states, in particular between Athens and Sparta. The country was finally unified under a Macedonian king. By 323 Alexander had conquered an immense empire stretching from the Adriatic Sea to the river Indus. But by 168 B.C. Greece had become a Roman province within the ever expanding empire.

Booklist

EARLY MAN *The Missing Link* by M.A. Edey (Time Life Books, 1972–73); *The Prehistory of Europe* by P. Phillips (Penguin Books, 1981); *The Evolution of Man* by J. Jelinek (Hamlyn, 1975); *Prehistoric Societies* by G. Clark, S. Piggott (Penguin Books, 1970); *The Evolution of Early Man* by B. Wood (Peter Lowe, 1976); *Spain and Portugal, the Prehistory of the Iberian Peninsula* by H.N. Savory (Thames and Hudson, 1968); *The Atlas of Early Man* by J. Hawkes (Macmillan, 1976) *Ancient Europe* by S. Piggott (Edinburgh University Press, 1973).
ÇATAL HÜYÜK *Çatal Hüyük: A Neolithic Town in Anatolia* by J. Mellaart (Thames & Hudson, 1967); *The Earliest Civilisation of the Middle East* by J. Mellaart (Thames & Hudson, 1971); *The First Cities* by D.J. Hamblin (Time Life, 1973).
ANCIENT EGYPT *The Rape of the Nile* by B.M. Fagan (Macdonald & Jane's, 1977); *The Ancient Egyptians: How They Lived and Worked* by J. Kamil (David & Charles, 1976).
MINOAN CRETE *Lost World of the Aegean* by M.A. Edey (Time Life Books, 1975); *Minoan and Mycenaean Art* by R. Higgins (Thames and Hudson, 1974); *The Arts in Prehistoric Greece* by S. Hood (Penguin Books, 1978).
PEOPLE OF THE NORTH *The Bronze Age in Europe (2,000–700 B.C.)* by J.M. Coles, A.F. Harding (Methuen, 1979).
ANCIENT CHINA *The Prehistory of China* by J.M. Treistman (David and Charles, 1972); *Ancient China* by P. Fitzgerald (Elsevier-Phaidon, 1978).
THE ETRUSCANS *The Etruscans* by D.J. Hamblin (Time Life Books, 1975); *Etruscan Art* by O.J. Brendel (Penguin Books, 1978); *Central and Southern Italy Before Rome* by D. Trump (Thames and Hudson, 1966).
ANCIENT GREECE *Life in Classical Athens* by T.B.L. Webster (Batsford, 1978); *The Greeks* by H.D. Kitto (Penguin, 1977).